Success!

THE ESSENTIAL PARENT GUIDE

MACMILLAN EDUCATION

THE WRITERS

DR ROGER MERRY
  Head of Primary Teacher Training at Leicester University (*Reading and Writing*)

DR DAVID LEWIS
  Writer and lecturer at Sussex University (*Psychological aspects of learning*)

WENDY BODY
  Writer of children's educational books
  Head of Avon Remedial Reading Services (*You and your child's school*)

DR ALAN PEACOCK
  Senior lecturer, Department of Education, University of Exeter (*Learning to solve problems*)

KEITH GAINES
  Special Needs adviser, Waterfield LEA and writer (*Dealing with anxiety*)

© Macmillan Education Ltd 1989

All rights reserved. No reproduction, copy or transmission of this publication may be made without written permission.

No paragraph of this publication may be reproduced, copied or transmitted save with written permission or in accordance with the provisions of the Copyright Art 1956 (as amended), or under the terms of any licence permitting limited copying issued by the Copyright Licensing Agency, 33–4 Alfred Place, London WC1E 7DP.
Any person who does any unauthorised act in relation to this publication may be liable to criminal prosecution and civil claims for damages.

First published 1989

Published by
MACMILLAN EDUCATION LTD
Houndmills, Basingstoke, Hampshire RG21 2XS
and London
Companies and representatives
throughout the world

Printed in Hong Kong

ISBN 0–333–46321–8

THE ADVISERS

Many parents and teachers have read and revised the material for this book. They include:
John Aldridge, Helen Arnold, Peter Batty, Jackie Brien, Miranda Carter, Norman Cawley, Tony Charlton, Ron Dawson, Alan Graham, Lena Joffe, David Kearney, Joan Miller, Antonia Murphy, Betty Prescott, Jo Rigby, Ken Tyler, Marnie Winterstein.

CO-ORDINATING EDITOR
Elizabeth Paren

DESIGNERS
Plum Design, Southampton

ACKNOWLEDGEMENTS
The publishers wish to thank the following for the photographs used in this book:
Jim Brownhill; Camera Press; Central Television; Chris Fairclough; Sally and Richard Greenhill; Paul Davies Pictures; Liba Taylor; Elizabeth Whiting & Associates; Diana Wyllie Ltd; ZEFA.

CONTENTS

This is *Success!* 4
Parents and teachers as partners 5
What is your role? 6

Helping your child learn how to learn 7

Listening to your child 8
Questions and answers 9
Improving your child's memory 10
Learning to solve problems 12
The skills of problem-solving 13
More problem-solving skills 14
Problem-solving at home 16
Helping your child want to learn 17

Getting the most out of Success! 19

How to get the most out of *Success!* 20
How well does your child read? 22
Reading — an essential tool 24
How can you help more? 26
Improving reading skills 28
How well does your child write? 30
Writing is hard work 32
What can you do about neatness and accuracy? 34
What can you do about content? 36
Mathematics for life 38

Maths can be enjoyed! 40
Maths — common sticking points 42
Choosing the right books 46

Your child's world 47

Dealing with anxiety 48
Relationships with other children 50
Your child's changing body 51
Building up your child's confidence 52
Encouraging independence 55
Dealing with group pressures 56
Managing the family's time 57
Making workspace for your child 58

You and your child's school 59

Meeting the teacher 60
The world of school 62
Choosing the right school 65
What do you do when things go wrong? 66
How to get more involved 68
Where to get further advice 70
Detailed assessment for your child 72
Where to find out about 72

THIS is SUCCESS!

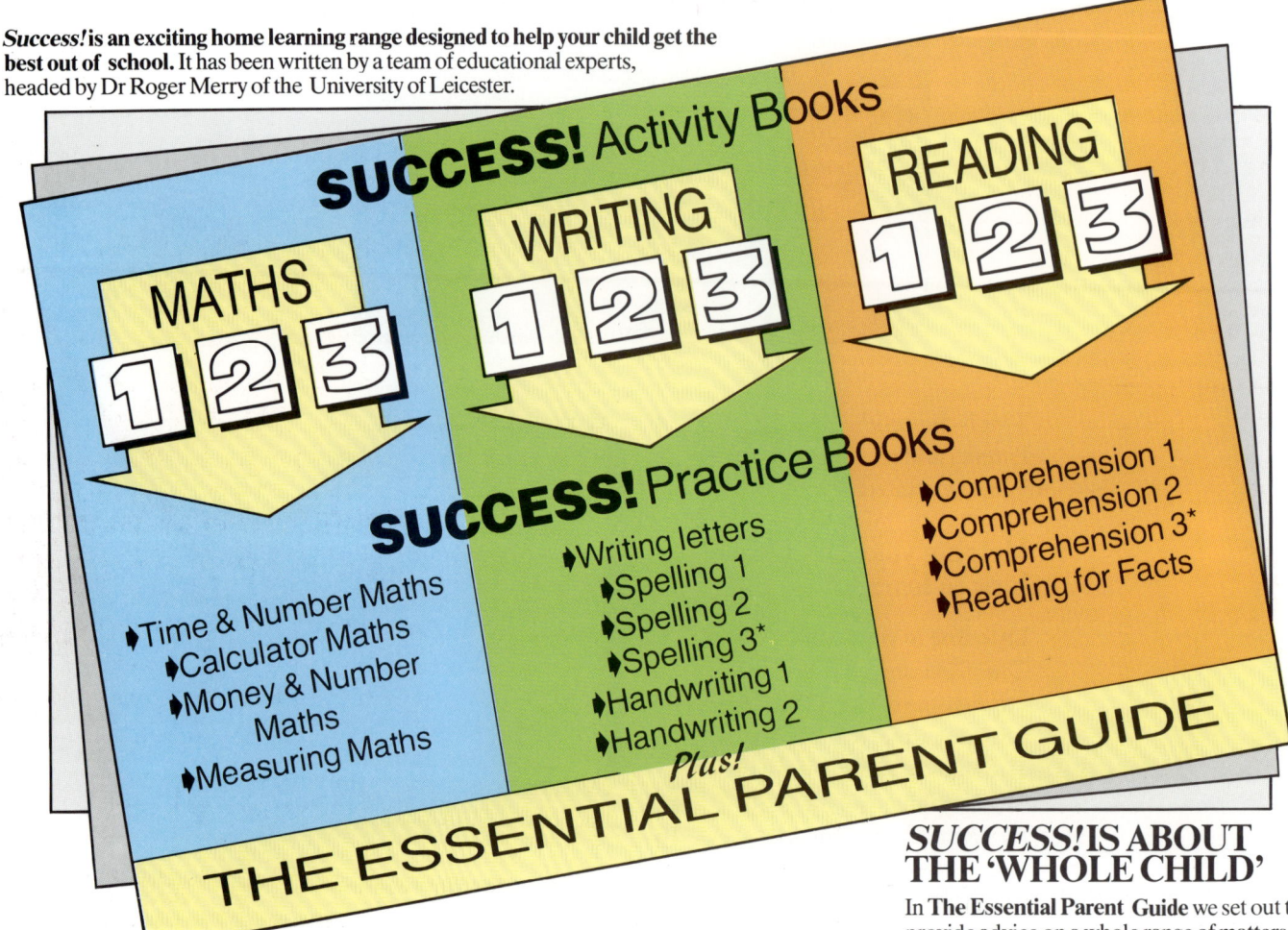

Success! is an exciting home learning range designed to help your child get the best out of school. It has been written by a team of educational experts, headed by Dr Roger Merry of the University of Leicester.

SUCCESS! Activity Books

MATHS 1 2 3
WRITING 1 2 3
READING 1 2 3

SUCCESS! Practice Books

- Time & Number Maths
- Calculator Maths
- Money & Number Maths
- Measuring Maths

- Writing letters
- Spelling 1
- Spelling 2
- Spelling 3*
- Handwriting 1
- Handwriting 2

- Comprehension 1
- Comprehension 2
- Comprehension 3*
- Reading for Facts

Plus!

THE ESSENTIAL PARENT GUIDE

* in preparation

ACTIVITY BOOKS

There are **Activity books** for each of the three main subjects, **maths, writing** and **reading**. There is a choice of three levels in each subject — it's a good idea to start with the first level in each subject and then see how much progress your child makes.

PRACTICE BOOKS

This is a series of books designed to improve specific skills which are part of each subject. Your child may need particular help with handwriting, for example.

The exercises in the **Practice books** are easier than those in the **Activity books**, but they are still lots of fun to do.

SUCCESS! MOTIVATES

Children are often enthusiastic about school and about learning when they are very young. By the time they are 9 or 10 their enthusiasm may be beginning to falter. They are finding some subjects interesting – others less so. *Success!* sets out to revive your child's enthusiasm and interest in the three most vital subjects.

SUCCESS! DEVELOPS SKILLS

A glance at the Contents pages (pages 6 and 7) of any of the **Activity books** will give you an idea of the skills we cover.

The *Success!* range dovetails with the latest requirements of the school curriculum, as well as stimulating the child's active participation in learning these skills.

SUCCESS! IS ABOUT THE 'WHOLE CHILD'

In **The Essential Parent Guide** we set out to provide advice on a whole range of matters – all of which affect your child's classroom performance. We offer guidance, for example, on how you can deal with such problems as anxiety and lack of confidence. We provide practical advice too on such things as choosing books for your child, and planning an effective study area.

SUCCESS! SUPPORTS TEACHERS

In **The Essential Parent Guide** you'll also find information which will enable you to be an active partner in your child's education. We discuss, for example, the implications of the **national curriculum** and other changes introduced by the Education Reform Bill of 1988. We stress throughout the importance of this partnership – between the professionally qualified teacher and the active and concerned parent. We see it as vital for your child's educational success.

PARENTS TEACHERS AS PARTNERS

Attitudes to education are changing – in rather the same way as attitudes to health care are changing. In the past, many people assumed it was their doctor's job to keep them healthy. They could eat what they wished and take very little exercise. It was the doctor's responsibility to give them the pills or potions to keep them fit. Now we accept that it is our responsibility to keep as healthy as possible – hence our enthusiasm for exercise bikes and healthy eating! It is much more a matter of collaborating with the doctor – and most doctors welcome this co-operation.

Similarly, most teachers welcome the increasing co-operation with parents. It is, of course, still up to the professionals to teach the specific skills of reading, writing and maths, for example. It is their job also to impart essential knowledge and help each child realise his or her potential. But they have many children to teach. **Try as they might, no teacher can give your child the individual attention that you as a parent can give.**

It's the job of the professional to teach basic skills and help each child realise his or her potential.

KNOWING AND FEELING

Classroom attainment is not just about intellect. It is also about your child's feelings. The attitudes that your child may have to learning are crucial to his success. Given two children of equal intelligence, one motivated and self-assured and the other apathetic and anxious, there will be no contest between them. The first will far outpace the second, despite their similar abilities.

> We, in the West, have tended to ignore the way children *feel* about their studies. However, the Chinese have, for centuries, appreciated the powerful role which the emotions play in successful learning. They realise that intelligence is a matter of both heart and head.

Skills and attitudes are inextricably linked. **All children have learning problems at some stage or other.** You can help them master the basic skills, by helping them adopt useful strategies for learning, by helping them want to learn – and above all by being there to encourage, praise and assist. Knowing that she has your interest, support and encouragement your child is likely to tackle her classroom learning with greater confidence and assurance – and her chances of educational success will be immeasurably improved.

PARTNERSHIP WORKS

Parents and teachers are working together more and more and children are benefiting. Many schools are adopting PACT schemes – Parents and Children Together. Within these schemes parents make a commitment to helping their child learn to read – they agree to spend some time each day doing paired or shared reading with their child. See page 29 for more information.

> **Some 75% of formal learning takes place through reading. This means that success in school, as well as enjoyment and understanding in later life, depend on reading fluency. Listening parents hold the key to children's literacy. Research has shown that the progress of children helped at home can exceed that of children helped by specialist teachers at school.**
>
> Report to House of Commons Select Committee by National Association for the Teaching of English, March 1986

This book is for parents of children between the ages of 9 and 12. Your child has probably learnt to read. You may feel that you have made your contribution by listening to him read each day and that now the teacher should take over. *Success!* insists that that valuable partnership between parents and teachers should continue – even when your child has left primary school.

WHAT WILL THE TEACHER THINK?

Success! does represent the best of current educational thinking and there should be no conflict between it and what happens in your child's classroom. Nevertheless you may be worried about what your child's teacher may think of it – after all the Activity and Practice books don't look anything like the textbooks your child brings home from school!

You may find it helpful to talk to the teacher about *Success!* Take the books in to show her or him. Explain why you've bought them, i.e. what it is that is worrying you about your child's school performance. The teacher will probably be pleased to discuss your child's problems with you.

Talk to the teacher again when your child has done some of the *Success!* books. You will have discovered some things about your child's learning – you will feel better informed when next you meet the teacher!

It must be stressed that *Success! in no way seeks to replace the professional skill of the teacher.* It does enable you as a parent to become a fully involved partner in the education of your child.

WHAT IS YOUR ROLE?

Are you concerned about your child's education? If you're reading this book, you probably are!

Are you thinking about buying a home learning scheme to help your child with school work? If so, do you have doubts about what *you* will have to do? Perhaps you feel you don't have the time or the expertise to help your child? In fact the most important thing is to **encourage your child**. It's a thing which comes naturally to a parent. So be on hand, be ready to give your undivided attention, be ready to help. (You'll find more detailed guidance on how to use the ***Success!*** books on pages 20 and 21.)

Your role is to encourage – not to criticise.

Do you feel the statement at the top of the page applies to you?

You can give your child the individual time and attention that no teacher has the time to give.

❋ The ***Success!*** books have been designed so that your child will enjoy using them on his own, with the minimum of help from you.

❋ Can you set aside a short period each day when you can be sure that you can be available to help your child? Work out the best time of day together.

❋ **It's better to plan for short, frequent sessions.** 15 to 20 minutes will often be enough.

❝ I can't pretend to be a teacher. After all, they have professional qualifications – I don't know the first thing about teaching.❞

❝ Yes, I am concerned about my child's education – but life seems so busy nowadays, I really haven't got the time to sit down and explain things to him.❞

❋ ***Success!*** is not intended to replace school lessons. The books have been specifically designed for use by children at home.

❋ You have a unique role to play – you can give the individual attention and encouragement that no teacher has time to give.

❋ By using ***Success!*** you'll help to improve your child's attitude to the work she does in the classroom – you're supporting the teacher, not trying to replace him.

❝ How do I know that these books fit in with what my child is doing at school?❞

❋ The majority of teachers support the idea of home learning.

❋ ***Success!* represents the best of current educational practice.** The emphasis of the school curriculum is increasingly towards problem-solving and the development of logical and flexible thinking skills. ***Success!*** reflects this emphasis throughout the range. (You'll find more about 'Problem-solving' on pages 12 to 16.)

❋ Improving your child's basic skills in reading, writing and maths can only help her school performance. Helping her to tackle school tasks with confidence and assurance will enable her to develop further and more sophisticated skills.

❝ The trouble is, whenever I do try to help my child I find myself getting impatient.❞

Yes, patience *is* important – but there are things you can do to lessen the chances of getting impatient.

❋ Remember that **learning is all about making mistakes.** Is there something that you have learnt to do recently – like driving, using a word processor, using a microwave? You probably made some mistakes before you learnt to do it perfectly.

❋ It does help if you are relaxed before you start helping your child. You'll have your own ways of relaxing – it may be sitting down with a cup of tea or even a large gin and tonic! It may be taking deep breaths or taking a walk round the garden. If you find it really difficult to relax there's a suggested method of relaxation on page 49.

❋ Impatience can be a sign that someone is worried. If you feel worried about not understanding the task, give yourself time to work through the activity carefully before you work with your child.

❝ I was hopeless at school – I really don't think I'm going to be much help.❞

❋ This attitude is probably better than an over-confident one! If you found school work difficult you're more likely to understand your child's problems.

❋ Many of us feel particularly inadequate when it comes to helping our children with maths. The ***Success!*** maths activities relate maths to everyday life, so they are not full of sums! Try going through some of the activities in a Maths Activity book yourself, before you give it to your child.

HELPING your CHILD LEARN HOW TO LEARN

Listening to your child	8
Questions and answers	9
Improving your child's memory	10
Learning to solve problems	12
The skills of problem-solving	13
More problem-solving skills	14
Problem-solving at home	16
Helping your child want to learn	17

M

LISTENING TO YOUR CHILD

Like most parents you probably don't listen to everything your child says – and let's face it, a lot of what children go on about doesn't need our full attention!

What matters is that we *do* listen when our children are trying to tell us something important. The trouble is, when something has happened at school which makes a child upset – when he is really worried about a piece of school work or nervous about a test, a new teacher or something similar – most children don't come rushing home to tell you about it.

It has probably happened in your family that suddenly one child starts behaving oddly – perhaps a normally well-behaved child really plays up, or a normally noisy one goes very quiet. *Only days afterwards do you realise that it was all to do with something that happened at school.*

In these situations it does help if you know how to listen carefully – not just to what you are told in words but to the hidden messages that are not conveyed in words at all. Careful listening is not the same as hearing – listening is a skill which can be learnt and practised.

HALF-LISTENING

This is the kind of listening we do most of the time. You think you are listening but really your mind is on other things. It's quite obvious to your child that you're not listening. Unless she jumps up and down, or does something to attract your full attention, she's likely to give up. Sometimes it might be possible to admit to your child that you're really not able to listen now – but you will listen later. If you do this, then *do* keep your promise.

NEUTRAL LISTENING

We're listening to the words, thinking about them and making sense of them. If all that is happening is an exchange of information then this can be the most appropriate form of listening. Children need to develop the skills of neutral listening as early as possible. It's an important way of acquiring information as much of their time in the classroom will be spent listening.

It's *not* an appropriate way of listening, though, if your child wants to tell you something important but can't put it into words. The actual words may convey one thing, the hidden messages of tone and body language may say something quite different.

'I'm not worried by the test tomorrow,' said Mary, who was, in fact, terrified and wanted to talk about it.
'That's good,' was her mother's cheerful response.

CAREFUL LISTENING

It's only by listening carefully that we can really understand what we're being told. This involves not only listening to the words, but picking up the messages conveyed by tone and body language.

Let's suppose you've noticed that something is wrong. Your child is not behaving normally and you want to know what's wrong. You ask, 'What's wrong?' The most likely answer is, 'Nothing.' Don't nag. Look for another opportunity to ask, or try to find out more indirectly.

ONCE YOUR CHILD *HAS* STARTED TALKING

Say as little as possible. *You may be dying to say something but keep it back if you can.* Try not to interrupt even if there is a silence – your child needs time to think.

Keep looking interested – and try not to show it if what your child is saying makes you angry or worried.

Pay attention to the tone of voice – does it seem to conflict with what your child is saying?

Notice any self-mocking jokes – they could be a sign that your child is worried or embarrassed.

Watch the expression, gestures and body language.

Notice if there are lots of pauses, hesitations or repetitions – again these may indicate anxiety or some other strong emotion.

Keep what you have been told to yourself – don't betray your child's trust. You'll want to talk about it with your partner but wait until there is no-one else around.

Body language signs

We're all more aware of body language these days. Looking for clues in the way a person moves can be helpful. It may enliven the next meeting or social gathering you go to!

All children will do *all* of these things sometimes. What you are looking for are body language signs which are *unusual* in your child.

Blocking child crosses arms or legs, avoids eye-contact, leans away. *Shows* embarrassment, anger, discomfort or worry.

Fidgeting scuffing shoes, playing with fingers or pencils, fiddling with clothes. *Shows* worry.

Picking or pulling at skin, hair, clothes, nose or, especially in small boys, genitals. *Shows* anxiety mainly but can be a sign of anger that is turned inwards.

Illustrating rhythmic hand and arm gestures used to accompany words and emphasise points. *Shows* confidence and assurance; watch in case these are replaced by blocking or fidgeting movements.

Maintaining eye-contact is a very subtle signal. Excessive eye contact *usually* indicates aggressive feelings.

Avoiding eye contact inappropriately *implies* embarrassment, anxiety or deceit.

QUESTIONS AND ANSWERS

Children learn a great deal through asking questions. They also spend a lot of time answering questions.

A considerable amount of classroom time is taken up by teachers asking questions. They do so to test knowledge, identify errors, correct misunderstandings and evaluate learning. And sometimes to make sure children are listening!

What sort of questions does your child have to answer in class? There are three main kinds of questions.

Listen to your child's views – and try to answer her questions.

QUESTIONS THAT TEST MEMORY

Most of the questions which are asked in the classroom test memory, or the ability to recall knowledge. Memory skills are important; children need to be able to remember tables, spellings and other facts and figures. You will find advice on how to improve your child's memory on pages 10 and 11.

QUESTIONS THAT TEST UNDERSTANDING

These are 'how?', 'why?', 'what for?' questions that are aimed at finding out whether what the child has in her memory has really been taken in.

PROBLEM-SOLVING QUESTIONS

These questions cannot be answered quickly. They require an understanding of the problem, the careful selection of relevant knowledge, the use of logical and creative thinking. It is **these skills** which are supremely important for your child – they **are the key to future educational success.** You will find a lot more about problem-solving on pages 12 to 16.

There are games you can play at home which will develop your child's ability to deal with more thought-provoking questions.

Behind the headlines

The whole family can join in this game.
Choose a story from the daily newspaper (or from radio or TV news bulletins). Use questions and answers to explore all the implications which might follow. You could take it to absurd lengths – make the game increasingly fantastic and amusing.

For example A headline about a major traffic jam on the motorway might trigger the question: *What would happen if none of the cars could ever move again?*

Build up a fantasy about people setting up home on the abandoned motorway, schools opening in stranded lorries, small gardens being planted on the bonnets of cars . . .

Make sure you're not the one asking the questions all the time. Get your child to ask you questions too. This could be a really good way to pass the time on a long train or car journey.

ANSWERING QUESTIONS IN CLASS

Does your child answer questions in class? Does she ask for help if she is not clear about something? You probably don't know the answers to these questions. Many children are very reluctant to speak up in class and there are all kinds of reasons.

The child may not want to make a mistake, may be fearful of criticism. She may be shy or may not want to stand out. She may feel that everyone else knows the answer except her or she may be reluctant to appear too clever in case the other children think she's showing off.

WHAT CAN YOU DO?

You can give your child lots of encouragement – give her the chance to participate in family decision-making, listen to her views seriously. Don't laugh when she does express a point of view.

Show your child that everyone makes mistakes – and that that's the way we learn. Tell her about mistakes you've made and show how you are able to laugh about them now.

HOW TO ANSWER YOUR CHILD'S QUESTIONS

Young children ask lots of questions. As they grow older these become less frequent, although they become more complicated. Curiosity has diminished. But so often children give up asking questions because they don't get given answers. Do try to find the time to answer your child's questions – it is one of the best ways of extending your child's knowledge.

REMEMBER

- **If you know** a lot about a subject, don't make your reply too rapid or apparently effortless. Go slowly. Otherwise the child may be over-awed by your mastery of the subject and consequently feel reluctant to ask you any more.

- **While solving** a problem, talk aloud about how you're doing it – and encourage your child to do the same.
- **Be prepared** to make deliberate mistakes – and then to correct them.
- **Encourage** your child to find answers for himself (see page 46 on building up a reference library).

- **And *don't*** come to hasty conclusions about what you are being asked. There was once a 7-year-old who asked his mother 'Where did I come from?' Embarrassed but prepared, she gave him a 20 minute talk on the birds and the bees, then asked if that answered the question. 'Not really. It's just that my friend says she comes from Liverpool!'

IMPROVING YOUR

As we mentioned on page 9 there are things which children have to remember. They need to know their tables, remember their spellings and, for subjects such as history, geography and science, there are facts to be learnt.

Although children spend most of their time in class being told what to learn, they are rarely taught *how* to learn. Lessons in remembering are not on any school timetable.

No-one really knows how the memory works. What we do know is that it is more difficult to remember things which we do not find interesting in themselves. On this page you will find some games and techniques which your child might find useful for improving her memory.

Did you know?

- Within the first five years of a child's life, he learns 50% of everything he'll ever know!
- By the late teens his memory will contain more information than can be found in the British Museum's library of *nine million* volumes.
- But it will never run out of space.
- Experts say your child's brain can store 11 new facts per second throughout life and still have ample reserves.

SPOT MESSAGES

This is a very effective way of learning the names of household objects in a foreign language. The words are written in red on slips of paper and are stuck up around the house. Post-it note pads, which will attach to virtually any surface without doing any damage, are ideal.

The words can be stuck onto appropriate items, for example *'une chaise'* could be stuck on a chair.

Every time your child glances at the spot message the word will become more deeply fixed in his memory.

MAKING A KNOWLEDGE TREE (OR CIRCLE OR...)

The most inefficient way to learn facts is to stare at a textbook. It is when we are *doing* something with the information, when learning is an *active* process, that the facts are most likely to be efficiently stored in the memory.

This technique can work well with any school subject where there are a lot of facts to learn, such as history or geography.

WHAT TO DO

1 Help your child collect together about 12 plain cards (about the size of postcards), and some coloured pens.

2 Together, select about 12 important facts on one particular topic (our illustration gives facts about cars). The facts can come from a textbook, a reference book or the notes your child has made in class.

3 Help your child write each fact on a card, writing as few words as possible, using different coloured pens for words, drawings, numbers, etc. You may find the section on note-taking on page 37 useful for this.

4 Discuss with your child the best way to arrange the cards on a table. You want to arrange them so that there is a connecting pattern. This might take the form of a tree as in our example. It could just as well take the form of a circle or a simple line.

5 Now turn all the cards, except one, face down. Can your child remember what it says on the card *next* to the one he can see? He can check the answer by looking at the card. Now ask if he can remember the facts on the *next* card to that one, and so on...

WHY THIS TECHNIQUE WORKS

- It involves active learning – **your child starts to remember the moment he starts writing** down the information on the cards. He is *doing* something, not just staring at the words on a page.

- It stores knowledge in several different memory locations: your child reads the information aloud (*sound memory*), writes it down (*word memory*) and creates images (*visual memory*).

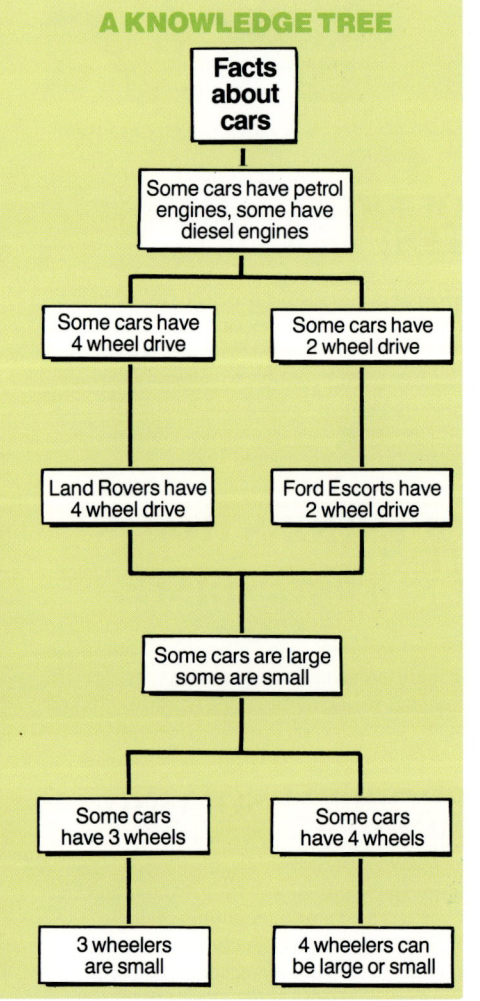

A KNOWLEDGE TREE

```
              Facts
              about
              cars
                │
     Some cars have petrol
     engines, some have
        diesel engines
         ┌──────┴──────┐
  Some cars have    Some cars have
   4 wheel drive     2 wheel drive
         │                │
  Land Rovers have  Ford Escorts have
   4 wheel drive     2 wheel drive
         └──────┬───────┘
         Some cars are large
         some are small
         ┌──────┴──────┐
   Some cars        Some cars
  have 3 wheels    have 4 wheels
         │                │
    3 wheelers       4 wheelers can
    are small       be large or small
```

CHILD'S MEMORY

THE LEARNING LADDER

This is another way of getting your child actively involved in learning. Organising information on a learning ladder like this can be a useful aid to memory.

1. Get a sheet of stiff card, about 75cm by 100cm (30″ × 36″).

2. Either draw rungs onto the ladder, or, preferably, stretch ribbons across. This allows the ladder to be more easily adjusted.

3. Key facts about the chosen topic should be written onto cards.

4. Arrange the facts on the ladder. It's a good idea to put more general information at the top, more detailed information near the bottom.

5. Additional information, in the form of notes, drawings, diagrams can be placed around the side of the ladder. They can be linked with the facts on the ladder by ribbons.

FACTS ABOUT TREES

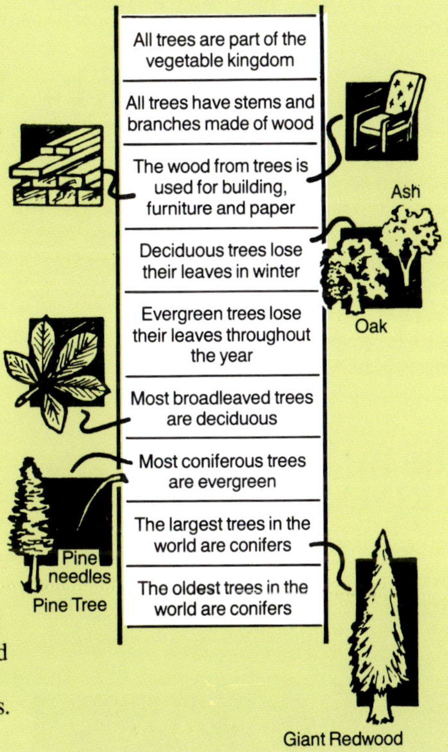

- All trees are part of the vegetable kingdom
- All trees have stems and branches made of wood
- The wood from trees is used for building, furniture and paper
- Deciduous trees lose their leaves in winter
- Evergreen trees lose their leaves throughout the year
- Most broadleaved trees are deciduous
- Most coniferous trees are evergreen
- The largest trees in the world are conifers
- The oldest trees in the world are conifers

Ash
Oak
Pine needles — Pine Tree
Giant Redwood

MNEMONICS

These aids to the memory are particularly effective when they are in verse.

> *Thirty days hath September, April, June and November…*

is one of the best known mnemonics.

One way of remembering the colours of the rainbow is by learning the sentence, 'Richard Of York Gave Battle In Vain' – that's easier than trying to remember the list of Red, Orange, Yellow, Green, Blue, Indigo, Violet.

Mnemonics can be useful for learning to spell difficult words. See page 34 for more information.

It's best if your child can make up her own mnemonics, but it takes practice. Be careful not to make them too complicated.

MAKE TAPES

You could help your child record the facts she needs to learn. She can play them at odd moments – if she has a personal cassette player she can listen to them even when brushing her teeth. This might be a good way for your child to learn tables! Some people even find it helps to sing or chant them! **Don't be embarrassed – try it, and if it works, use it!**

REMEMBERING BY PLACE

This is a very ancient technique.

WHAT TO DO

1. Walk round the house and choose places to 'put' the facts.

2. Take the list of facts to be remembered. Now walk round and imagine 'putting' each in one of the places you chose.

3. To recall the list, simply walk through the house and 'retrieve' each item placed there.

4. This technique could be used for a whole range of school subjects. Key dates, or other figures could be imagined written up, in red ink, on the walls or even on the ceilings of different rooms.

This may sound crazy, but try it yourself. It really works!

REMEMBER

- Don't allow negative comments like, 'I've got a terrible memory…'
- Do encourage your child to organise facts efficiently
- Do help your child to link the facts he needs to remember – this will aid rapid and accurate recall
- Do use images as well as words wherever possible
- Do involve your child actively in her learning

TV quiz programmes emphasise the importance of being able to remember facts.

11

Learning to SOLVE PROBLEMS

THE IMPORTANCE OF PROBLEM-SOLVING

Most of us can recognise a problem when we see one. They come up every day – what to have for lunch, how to keep healthy, when to buy new shoes for the children, why the bell won't work, and so on. Problems come in all sorts and sizes; some are never solved, some depend on other people, some are social, emotional, financial or physical.

CHILDREN AND PROBLEM-SOLVING

Lots of problems can be solved by thinking carefully about them, or by doing something positive. It is this type of problem which children can learn to solve. Clearly there is no magic formula for solving problems, but there are skills which are useful, such as logical reasoning, searching for information, planning, trying alternatives, designing, modifying, adapting. Most of these can be learnt. Modern trends in education encourage the development of these skills. communications all changing at an ever increasing pace, teachers and employers are recognising that these skills are essential to all of us, both at work and in our daily domestic lives.

PROBLEM-SOLVING IN SECONDARY SCHOOLS

Problem-solving has been built into the curriculum of most secondary schools. Developments such as the government-funded Technical and Vocational Education Initiative (TVEI) and programmes like the Certificate in Pre-Vocational Education (CPVE) are followed by large numbers of pupils. New ways of recording pupils' achievements deliberately assess these skills.

PROBLEM-SOLVING IN PRIMARY SCHOOLS

Gradually, through the increased emphasis on maths and science in primary schools, problem-solving has become accepted as part of what all young children need as well. The best primary teachers have always made use of problem-solving. *'It's simply good primary practice,'* as one teacher pointed out.

They have always encouraged their children to follow instructions and visual clues, make models, draw diagrams, work out what was needed to make something, investigate objects with all their senses, search for explanations – the list is endless.

ASSESSING PROBLEM-SOLVING SKILLS

Under the new Education Act of 1988, all primary children will be assessed at ages 7 and 11. The skills of problem-solving will be assessed through the system of **attainment targets**, which prescribe essential skills to be learnt.

Here's an example of a maths problem-solving activity for 10 to 11-year-olds – the kind of thing which might be the basis for assessment.

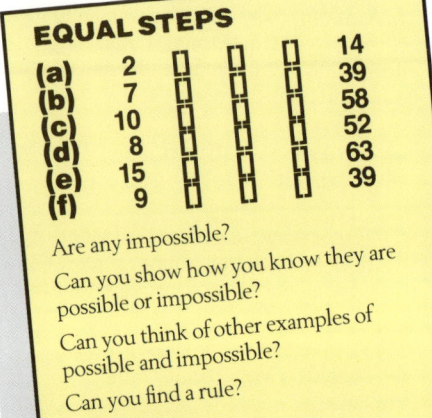

EQUAL STEPS

(a)	2 ☐ ☐ ☐	14
(b)	7 ☐ ☐ ☐	39
(c)	10 ☐ ☐ ☐	58
(d)	8 ☐ ☐ ☐	52
(e)	15 ☐ ☐ ☐	63
(f)	9 ☐ ☐ ☐	39

Are any impossible?

Can you show how you know they are possible or impossible?

Can you think of other examples of possible and impossible?

Can you find a rule?

Make a poster.

This is taken from a CEDTE publication, Leicester. The original came from Seaton Junior School, Cumbria.

Problem-solving should be fun!

This is why your child's teacher may use project work or activities like building bridges out of newspaper. They may not seem immediately relevant but they are developing these skills in the children.

The skills involved in solving problems which come up in school are the same skills which are invaluable for solving problems in real life. With technology, design and

Here is what some parents said about teaching maths through problem-solving, after they had worked for several days alongside their own children and their teachers in school.

❝ *The most important fact to us is that the children enjoyed it. It did not always follow that the more able children coped best. Less able children, and in fact all children, had more confidence to ask if they did not understand. When we asked the children the questions, 'What are you doing? How? Why?' they were able to answer positively. The fact that they were enjoying the work meant that they were learning from it. As parents we have had the feedback, 'Oh, it's Tuesday – good!' not 'Oh, it's Tuesday. Oh no, not maths all day.* ❞

Parent Governors' Report, Seaton Junior School, Cumbria

So the message about problem-solving, like the *Success!* series as a whole, is that it should be fun!

The Skills of PROBLEM-SOLVING

By now you may be worried that you simply don't know enough about all this to be of any help. Relax! It's not what you know that matters. It is a common feeling that, as parents or teachers, we ought to know the answers. In problem-solving, though, **knowing the answers can be a real handicap**. Here is an example to explain why.

The practical problem

It's breakfast time. Owen can't get the lid off a new pot of jam. He's got a real practical problem. So mum tries to do it. (Every family has a pet method! Running it under a hot tap; prizing it off with a knife; making holes in the lid; trapping it in the door jamb, . . .)

There are two snags here. First, mum's method may not work. Second, even if mum's method does work, Owen hasn't really learnt anything, except dependency. Worse, he probably assumes there is only one answer, which is obviously not true.

Recognising the problem

Here are two ways Owen might have put the problem to mum. Which would be more helpful?

Mum! I can't get this lid off!

What could be making this lid stick?

This is the first essential skill. Having recognised the real problem, the knack is to express it in a way that can be solved. One of Owen's options leads him to look for causes of the problem and think about what to do next. That's a good start to solving any problem, because it sets out a clear goal.

Looking with a purpose

Owen's question made him look at the jam pot for clues. This is a vital skill in solving many problems.

Looking with a purpose, or observing, is the second skill.

Transferable skills are so much more useful than isolated facts, too. The Chinese have a proverb for it.

Give me a fish and I eat for a day;
Teach me to fish and I eat for a lifetime.

Fish are isolated facts. Fishing is a skill.

YOU DON'T NEED TO KNOW THE ANSWER

Recognising and observing are just two examples of problem-solving skills; more are given below. The important thing is that you don't *need* to know how to unstick the jam pot lid. What you *do* need to do is to get your child to look at the problem in a useful way: observe closely and think of a few possible solutions which might work. The secret is not to rush at the first idea which pops into mind. There may actually be an easier way to do it and (better still) you and your child may find it together.

Developing your problem-solving skills

If you've never tried this kind of thing, try this problem, to get the feel of it.

❝ *What is the thickness of the page of this book that you are reading?* ❞

Work at it right now. No, there's no answer at the bottom of the page! We'll come back to it on page 16. Remember:

state the problem in a useful way,

observe everything closely,

think up a few alternative ways of solving the problem.

13

More

PLANNING A BATHROOM

This is a practical problem from a maths scheme used in many schools.

> *Imagine that you work for a large building firm and have to design various bathrooms for houses on a new estate. To do this, cut out the shapes of the bath, shower, washbasin, toilet, etc. and arrange them on the scale plan of the bathroom.*

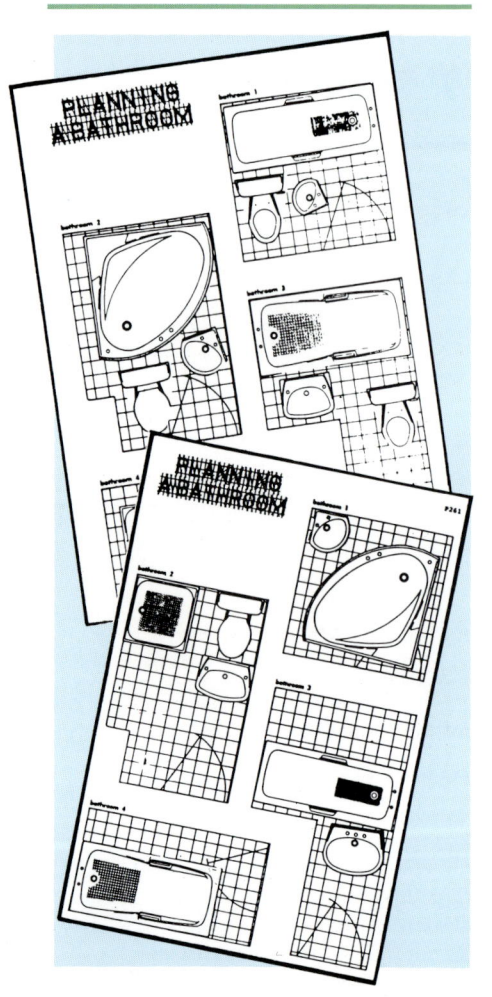

This involves various skills.

Logic skills: making sure that each bathroom has one bath, one basin, one toilet; trying various alternatives; seeing when these are the same or different; predicting what the room will look like.

Measuring skills: recognising the approximate size of a centimetre, a metre (or an inch, a foot); working out the size of floor tiles; calculating how much floor-space each item occupies.

Spatial skills: recognising when things are straight or at right angles; manipulating shapes so that they fit; relating the models or drawings to the real thing; making sure the door is not blocked.

WHICH IS THE BEST GLUE?

Science is now a compulsory 'core' subject for all primary children. Perhaps more than any other subject, science lends itself to problem-solving as a way of working, since the skills are more or less the same. Here is Rachel, trying to solve a typical science problem.

Rachel is making a model plane from lolly sticks...

WHAT SHE IS DOING	WHAT SHE IS SAYING
sticking two lolly sticks together with glue	"how can I find out which glue sticks best?"
holding two *different* tubes of glue	"all glues stick wood, I suppose, but some must stick stronger..."
holding the glued sticks and thinking	"I might try pulling them apart, or perhaps flying them and seeing which breaks easiest..."
clamping sticks to desk, and hanging a weight on the end	"I'll hang different weights on – that will be the most accurate way."
watching sticks break apart, weight falling	"this took only 50 grams to break the sticks..."
Holding separate sticks, thinking	"But I'm not sure I used the same amount of glue each time, so..."

You can see how Rachel went through several steps and used various skills.

Steps	*Skill used*
1: Recognising the problem 'How can I find out...?'	Asking questions
2: Being aware of what you already know 'All glues stick...'	Applying knowledge Predicting
3: Thinking of alternative solutions 'I might pull them apart...'	Generating strategies
4: Choosing and designing an investigation 'I'll hang weights...'	Making a 'fair test'
5: Carrying it out and seeing what happens 'This took 50 grams...'	Manipulating materials Observing Measuring
6: Evaluating her method 'But I'm not sure...'	Drawing conclusions Modifying Asking questions

So with this last question, the problem-solving cycle begins again for Rachel. In this way **your own child will invent or find many problems to solve**, problems which are of genuine concern to herself. So you won't always be having to think of new things for your child to do!

PROBLEM-SOLVING *Skills*

Right now, my 9-year-old son, having discovered brass-rubbing, is doing rubbings of tiles in the bathroom, trying to make new patterns by overlaying them. He is talking to himself:

'How can I…?'   *'Let's see if…'*   *'What about…!'*   *'Great!!'*

None of this was anybody's idea but his own.

The following summary chart lists all the main problem-solving skills, and where and how they may be used in school subjects.

Skills	Example	Relevant subject
Logic	seeing when things are in the correct sequence	all subjects
Measuring	finding how many floor tiles cover a square metre (or foot)	maths, science
Spatial	fitting shapes together, maps, scales	maths, art, geography
Asking questions	what happens if . . .	all subjects
Observing	looking, touching with a purpose	all subjects
Applying knowledge	making constructions	maths, science, technology, art
Predicting	if I do this, then . . . will happen	maths, science, technology, history
Making a 'fair test'	controlling all the things which can be varied except the one you are testing (type of glue)	science, technology
Evaluating	seeing if a model plane flies or not, deciding whether something works properly	maths, science, technology, history
Modifying	improving the design of something, trying to calculate differently	maths, science, technology, languages

CHILDREN'S PROBLEM-SOLVING STYLES

Like adults, children think in many different ways. Very often **there isn't just one 'right' way to answer a problem.**

On holiday in France, I was watching a group of children play 'Boule'. When there was a dispute about whose boule was nearest to the cochonner (the 'jack') they measured the distances. Each child had a different way of measuring. One used his feet; another used her hands; yet another estimated; a fourth used string.

Psychologists sometimes refer to **convergent** and **divergent** thinking, as two extremes of thinking style.

Convergent thinkers
Tackle problems methodically
Avoid guesswork and hunches
Analyse information carefully
Follow one line of thought at a time
Are thorough and logical

Divergent thinkers
Favour intuition over logic
Work rapidly, using inspired guesswork
Don't analyse systematically
Are highly imaginative and creative
Generate lots of ideas

Of course, most people are a mixture of the two. One style isn't necessarily better than the other. A lot depends on the nature of the problem.

How does your child solve problems?

❝ Make a paper aeroplane of your own design and try to fly it. ❞

Keep the questions below in mind as you observe (practise the skill of observing with a purpose). Did your child:

work methodically or by 'inspired hunches'?

become obsessed with one solution, or try several?

talk about what he was doing, or work in silence?

see what the real problem was, or not?

ask other questions, of you or of himself?

PROBLEM-SOLVING At Home

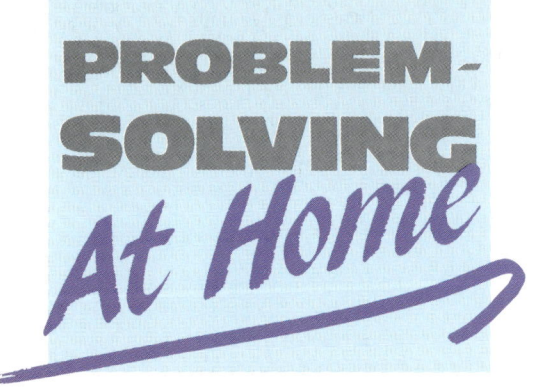

RECOGNISING PROBLEMS

Set your child simple, everyday problems as they occur at home. For example, how many buckets of water will we need to fill the paddling pool? How are we going to empty it? Which market stall gives the best value for oranges? How much do we owe the milkman?

Talk about what you're doing as you do it and encourage your child to do the same. For example, if you were helping Owen unstick his jam pot lid, you might say, 'We need to dissolve these sugar crystals round the top, so how can we do it? Let's try holding it under the tap.'

Give your child time to play around with a problem. Don't expect answers right away.

When discussing things with your child, formulate the problem yourself in different ways. For example, you might say, *'In other words, we need to...'*

Take an interest in your child's problems and work at them together. Ask questions about her hobbies, collections...

OBSERVING

Play quizzes and observation games regularly.

Encourage your child to draw, paint or model real things from life. Beware, though, if someone gives your child the modelling compound which sets in the oven. You never know what you will find next to the Sunday dinner!

Use lenses, microscopes, binoculars, cameras and other optical instruments which need careful adjustment and concentration. Even just looking down a tube can focus attention amazingly.

When your child is writing or drawing, focus his attention by asking questions such as, 'How many...? What colour...? What happens when...?'

FINDING ALTERNATIVE SOLUTIONS

Don't show frustration when your first attempt fails. Take time yourself. If the jam pot lid doesn't come off under the hot water, don't say, 'What a nuisance! Why don't

Games

I Spy
An old favourite, but it can be varied by giving different clues:
'I spy ... something cold and wet.'
'I spy ... something stripey.'
'I spy ... something hexagonal.'
etc.

Feely bags
An object is hidden in a bag or pillow case and has to be identified by touch.

Noisy tins
Objects are put inside tins (the sort with removable lids) and have to be identified by the type of rattle they make.

Blind Pugh
Someone closes his eyes and describes any familiar object, from memory. Someone else listens – possibly with her eyes closed too – and guesses the object.

you try the marmalade.' Try saying, instead, 'My hand is slipping. Perhaps I could hold it with a cloth.'

Ask your child to make something from the construction kit which is *not* in the manual: for example, a hang-glider, a dinosaur, a stage-coach.

Don't give your child final answers. Instead, ask, 'What are you actually doing? What else could you try? Why doesn't it work? Have you tried...?'

Save things which your child might find useful – not just yogurt pots and toilet-roll tubes. Look out for movable/flexible/compressible things (foam, tubing, polystyrene packing pieces, etc.).

DESIGNING AND CARRYING OUT INVESTIGATIONS

Encourage your child to make things herself rather than buying them, whenever possible. Home-made birthday cards and pencil cases can be fun to make (and receive). Point out that such creative skills are useful in everyday life, and save money!

Use questions starting, 'How could you find out...' whenever a suitable opportunity arises. For example:
- which is the most popular breakfast cereal?
- which way the wind blows most often?
- what most houses are made from?
- which room in the house is coolest/warmest?
- how fast other cars on the road are travelling?

Display the results of your child's problem-solving attempts. Ask him to tell you what he has found out, and how he solved the problem.

Above all, don't ignore your child's questions. He may be pestering you just when you don't want him to, but try not to dismiss him. 'That's a good question. Let me think about it,' is better than nothing.

How did you measure the thickness of the page?

You will have recognised that the real problem is how to measure something which is very thin or small. You will also have realised that the book is made up of many identical pages. You may have considered a number of different ways.

? Use a micrometer – but perhaps you don't have one.

? Fold it many times, divide the total thickness by the number of layers – but that involves tearing the page out of the book.

? Measure the total thickness of all the pages in the book, then divide by the number of leaves.

You may have decided that the first and last options are the most accurate, but that the last one is the quickest and simplest. You're probably right. **You see, you have all the skills needed to help your child.**

HELPING YOUR CHILD WANT TO LEARN

Motivation is essential to all school achievement. When well motivated, a child will have the enthusiasm and confidence to overcome almost any obstacles to learning. Without motivation even the brightest child is unlikely to enjoy much classroom success.

All children start off being highly motivated. A young child is naturally curious about his world – he wants to find out about everything. Hence the string of never-ending questions!

Young children at primary school are also usually keen to learn. The world is an immensely exciting place! As children get older, sometimes this natural curiosity gets inhibited. They may ask far fewer questions – perhaps because they get so few answers (see page 9).

For the 9 to 12-year-old child, school may no longer be so exciting. There may be subjects which she finds boring or difficult – there may be teachers whom she dislikes. Unless she finds a subject intrinsically interesting it may be hard for her to maintain her previous levels of enthusiasm. Of course, **teachers** go to considerable efforts to make their lessons stimulating and lively. But they **can't interest all of the children all of the time.**

HOW CAN YOU RECOGNISE LOW LEVELS OF MOTIVATION?

They are actually not easy to recognise but your answers to these questions may give you some clues.

- Does your child complain of being bored by school work?
- Does he give up too easily?
- Does he seem to lack confidence about his work at school?
- Does the standard of his school work seem to be going down?
- Does he seem to be worried about school?

WHAT CAN YOU DO?

◇ Could you take more interest in what your child is doing at school? It may be that your attention and interest could on their own be enough to revive your child's enthusiasm.

◇ *Praise and encouragement do help to build up a child's confidence.* Try to stop yourself criticising your child's work.

◇ By listening carefully to your child (see page 8) try to find out if he is having learning problems in a particular subject. This might be the case if your child seems to be 'turned off' by a subject he previously liked. If you suspect learning difficulties, talk to the teacher. (→)

Setting goals

1 Talk to your child about the subject you are going to tackle together. It should be one of those in which your child is showing little interest.

2 Decide together on a *goal.* This should be an objective which your child thinks she *can* achieve, and which she considers *worth achieving.* (Talk to your child's teacher about the goal you are setting.)

3 Try not to force your own ideas of what your child *should* be able to achieve – listen to her carefully and agree on a *realistic* goal.

4 As an example, you might have chosen to set the goal of getting better marks in a weekly maths test. Your child is currently only getting 20%. You would like her to be getting 90%. The two of you agree on a realistic target of 40%.

5 You could agree on a suitable reward but be careful about agreeing to give a much wanted present. If your child doesn't achieve the goal, the disappointment will be even harder to bear. It's much better to give a small reward as quickly as possible than to promise a big reward in the future.

6 Remember that if your child does achieve the goal her real reward will be the pleasure at having mastered something which she previously thought was beyond her grasp. It is this satisfaction with a job well done which is the key to motivation.

Family visits to places of historical interest can make history lessons come alive.

◇ Is your child having problems with a particular teacher? Sometimes a sarcastic teacher can badly affect a child's confidence. It might be useful to check with other parents on this. You might need to talk to the school head.

◇ Whatever you do, don't punish your child for apparent failure. This could further undermine his confidence.

◇ You could try using the **Success!** Activity and Practice books. The humour in the books is intended to catch your child's attention – to give him an incentive for doing the activities. Once he is doing the activities he will be thinking and learning.

◇ You might like to work out a specific programme with your child for tackling particular problems presented by certain subjects. *See the box on page 17.*

THE DANGERS OF OVER-MOTIVATION

It might seem that the more highly motivated your child the better. In fact the opposite can be true. Excessive motivation can be just as handicapping as too little.

You probably remember some time in your life, perhaps when going to an important job interview or going out with someone for the first time, **when you tried so hard to succeed that the whole event was a disaster.** There are times when the wish to succeed can interfere with normal thought processes. You might like to do *The bee and the cyclists* – it will demonstrate what we mean.

IS YOUR CHILD AFRAID OF FAILURE?

A common reason for counter-productive over-motivation is that a child is frightened of failing. Your child may be trying too hard – not because he seeks the satisfaction of achievement, but because failure is so frightening.

This might be the case if your child, for example, seems very reluctant to have a go at new things, or if he seems worried by a new teacher's different way of teaching.

Sometimes *you* might be the reason! Perhaps you find it very difficult to accept failure. Perhaps you are expecting too much of your child.

Remember that most children's levels of motivation vary from time to time and from subject to subject. If your child is really interested in one or two subjects then do as much as you can to encourage that interest. **Try to focus on the successes more than the failures.**

The bee and the cyclists

Please note before you do this, that your IQ level is indicated by the time it takes you to come up with an answer.

6 seconds or less = very intelligent
7-10 seconds = average
10-15 seconds = poor
more than 15 seconds = very low level of intelligence.

Two cyclists, one American and one British, face one another on a straight, cobbled, road 20 miles apart. At the same instant they start pedalling towards one another doing a steady 10 m.p.h.

There is a bee on the handlebars of the American's bike. The moment the bike starts to move, the bee takes off and flies to the handlebars of the oncoming British bike. Then he immediately flies back to the American bike. He continues to do this, covering the ever decreasing distance at a steady 15 m.p.h.

Assuming no time is lost in turning round at the end of each flight, what distance will the bee have covered by the time the two cycles meet?

Did you solve the problem?

The answer is 15 miles. The only relevant information is the distance and the speeds. The cyclists will meet in just one hour – the bee flies at 15 m.p.h.

All the other information was superfluous. And take no notice of those IQ ratings. They are completely fictitious and were put there only to increase your motivation to succeed. By doing so it is likely that your ability to select the relevant information was impaired.

What about getting her involved in a challenging physical activity?

Other ways that you can help

1 One way of improving motivation is to encourage challenging and interesting out-of-school activities. These must, obviously, be within your child's capabilities – but they should be sufficiently demanding to make success something to be proud of. Such activities could be hobbies, such as chess, computer games, painting, photography or playing a musical instrument. There are also more physical activities which are likely to build your child's confidence. What about getting her involved in roller-skating, running, swimming, football, canoeing, rock climbing? And – although the idea may horrify you – what about *you* getting involved in it too? If you don't like the idea of it, try to think why. It might help you to understand your child's reluctance.

2 You could also look for ways to link your child's out-of-school enthusiasms with school work. You'll get some ideas on pages 26-37 and 45.

GETTING THE most OUT OF SUCCESS

How to get the most out of *Success!*	20
How well does your child read?	22
Reading – an essential tool	24
How can you help more?	26
Improving reading skills	28
How well does your child write?	30
Writing is hard work	32
What can you do about neatness and accuracy?	34
What can you do about content?	36
Mathematics for life	38
Maths can be enjoyed!	40
Maths – common sticking points	42
Choosing the right books	46

M

HOW TO GET THE MOST OUT OF SUCCESS!

There are three extremely important ways in which you can generally help your child when she is learning at home.

Show interest in what your child does. You could ask her to explain what she is doing. You could even pretend not to understand. This will help you both check whether she really understands what she is doing. If you come across something neither of you can do, *try looking it up or working it out together.* This is a valuable experience for your child because it shows her that she is not the *only* one who gets stuck. It can also help her find ways of overcoming the problem.

Praise his efforts if you think he has tried. Indicate specifically any good points you can, rather than making general comments such as, 'That's lovely, Justin.' Almost all children want to please their parents, even though it may not always seem that way.

Encourage him to carry on. Again, you can make specific suggestions about what to do next, but do try to avoid telling your child what to do. **He'll be much more keen if he thinks it is his idea in the first place!**

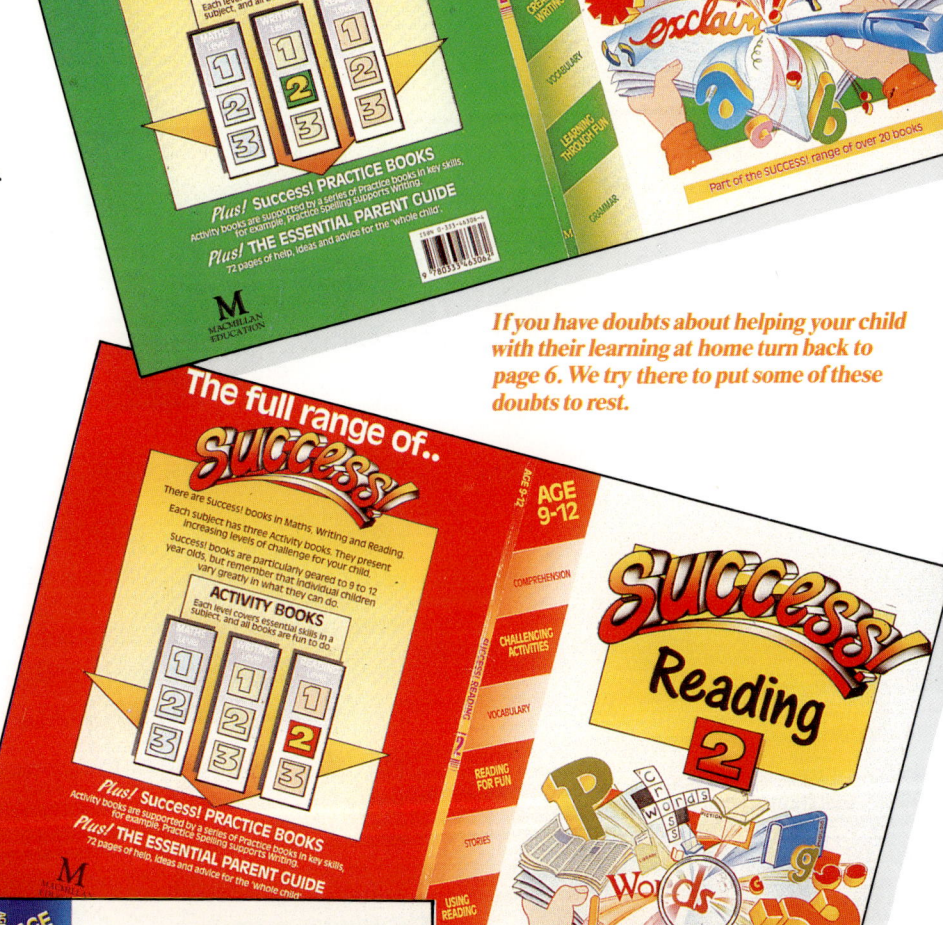

If you have doubts about helping your child with their learning at home turn back to page 6. We try there to put some of these doubts to rest.

WHERE TO START

The whole range of **Success!** books is particularly designed for children of about 9-12, although there will be many children outside this age range who could enjoy and benefit from them.

ACTIVITY BOOKS

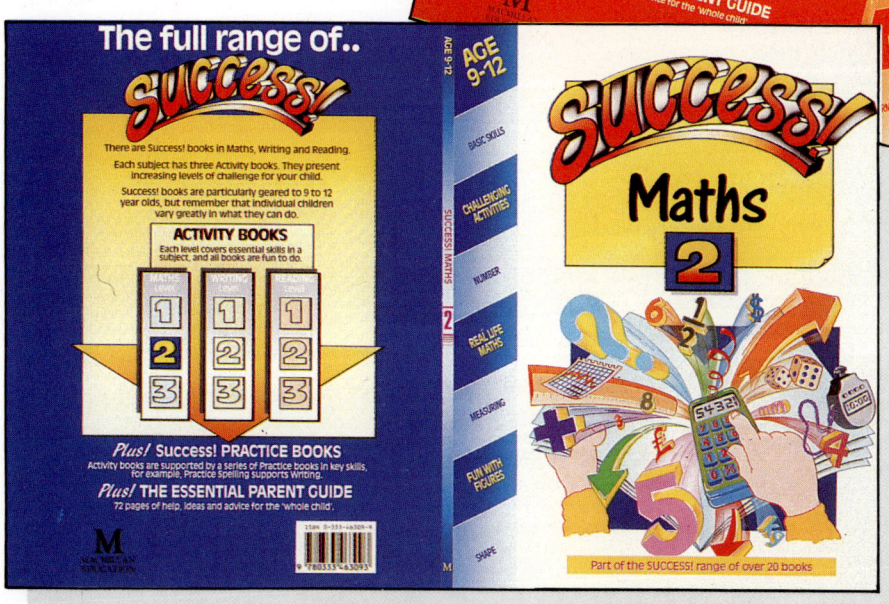

The nine **Activity books** are roughly divided into three levels, with three books each on the basic skills of maths, reading and writing. If you're not sure which level is best for your child we suggest you start with Level 1. Then you can move on to Levels 2 and 3 as your child seems ready. Even if he finds Level 1 quite easy, he'll still enjoy the activities and gain confidence from doing them. Each book covers a wide range of topics, enough to keep him interested.

When you get the book home, sit down together and have a look through it. Your child doesn't have to start at page 1 and work his way through the whole book. You could start one or two activities together, just to get the feel of them – enjoy the crazy characters and the daft situations. Then let your child choose the activity he wants to do. Once he's involved with it, say you'd like to see it when it's finished – then you can go and do something else.

> *You don't have to be there constantly, breathing down your child's neck.*

If your child knows that you are available when she needs you, that you are interested in what she is doing, she will find that in itself very encouraging. Research suggests that parents simply showing interest in their children's work is one of the most powerful factors in success at school.

When your child comes to show you what she's done, praise the effort she has made – this, in itself, is valuable. Then find something you can praise in what she has done. Try not to criticise.

See if she wants to do more now. Don't push it, if she seems to have had enough. ***It's better to have frequent, short sessions than to let it get boring.***

On the Contents page of the **Activity books** there are spaces for your child to tick the activities he has done. Encourage him to do this – **share the sense of achievement!**

In all the **Activity books** there is also a '*Success!* Awards Ceremony' page. When your child seems to have tried most of the activities in the book, encourage him to do this page. What he writes will help you see where he thinks he is having problems.

PRACTICE BOOKS

These will be particularly useful for children who seem to have specific problems in the three main areas – for example, with spelling or money maths. In general, the **Practice books** are rather more basic than the **Activity books** but they are still based on the *Success!* principles of thinking, learning and enjoying.

At this stage you may not know if your child has such specific problems. On the following pages you'll find suggestions as to how to assess your child's reading (pages 22-23) and writing (pages 30-31) and how to determine where your child is getting stuck in maths (pages 42-45).

HOW WELL DOES YOUR CHILD READ?

WHY DOES YOUR CHILD READ?

Does your child read for his own satisfaction and enjoyment – or does he tend to regard reading as something to be done for the teacher? See pages 26 and 27 on ways to improve reading attitudes.

To carry out these assessment activities your child will need to choose a book to read from. It might be one he's reading at the moment, or it might be one he's using at school. The important thing is that it is his choice.

You will also need to choose your moment. Choose a time when you know you can *both* be relaxed.

Don't feel you have to do everything at once. Break the sessions up – and take notice if your child says he has had enough.

ATTITUDES TO READING

Start by asking your child to read a couple of pages of the book out loud. How does your child react? His reactions will tell you something about his attitudes to reading. For example, **is he obviously reluctant, or eager to begin?** You'll find suggestions for improving your child's reading confidence on pages 26 and 27.

READING ALOUD

SOME POINTS TO NOTICE

1 If your child makes mistakes while reading, but carries on regardless, don't interrupt and correct her. Do the mistakes make sense? (For example, reading 'no-one' instead of 'nobody' here.) This kind of mistake suggests that your child isn't reading each word in turn, but is giving meaning to the text, which is what fluent readers do.

2 If your child gets stuck on a word, what does she do? Does she give up and wait for you to tell her? Try to give her clues first.

Does she have a guess? If so, does the guess make sense in the context of the sentence, or is it obviously wrong? Has your child perhaps only looked at the first letter? (For example, reading 'said' instead of 'sign' here.) If so, your child needs help in picking up clues from the context – she will benefit from some of the 'individual words' activities in the **Success!** Reading books.

---

train rattled off into the distance. David was left alone on the dusty platform. The sun beat down on his bare head and the heat shimmered over the railway tracks.

He looked round, puzzled. There was nobody there. No porter, no ticket collector, no Aunt to welcome him. Suddenly, David felt very much alone.

He picked up his suitcase and walked slowly towards the exit. He held his ticket ready in his hand, but still nobody appeared. At the exit, he paused, uncertain, then walked out into the road.

An old wooden sign pointed up the hill. It said, 'Chiltern Green ½ mile'. Chiltern Green was where his Aunt lived. He looked round. There was no sign of anybody.

David sighed and set off slowly up the road. He was really fed up. Why had he come here? As he walked, he kicked stones, scuffing his shoes and raising the dust. His suitcase was rubbing his fingers, so he changed hands. It didn't help much.

The half mile to the village seemed to take ages. Finally as he reached the top of the hill, there was the house. It was on the left, just as his Aunt had described it in her letter. 'Rose Cottage' – an old white house with a blue door.

He opened the gate and walked up the path. The garden was very overgrown, with long grass and weeds everywhere. He put down his case and knocked at the front door. He waited but there was no answer. He knocked again, louder this time. Still no answer. For the first time, he began to feel a bit scared.

He picked up his case and walked round the side of the house. The dustbin was tipped over, with rubbish all over the path. He stepped round the rubbish, setting flies buzzing angrily, and peered in through the window.

It was dark inside, but he saw at once that the room was completely bare. Where could his Aunt be? It was then that he noticed that the back door had been smashed off its hinges.

He felt really frightened now. There was

3 Does your child read with expression, or in a rather dull, flat voice, reading most words accurately but with little feeling? (For example does this sound like a question?) Does she pay attention to the pauses indicated by full stops and commas? See 'Punctuation' on page 35 for how you can help.

REMEMBERING

Reading aloud, though a useful way of estimating how well a child can read, is a rather special skill. What really matters is how well he's *understood*. One way of finding this out is to ask him to recall what he's read. If he's started a story, you can ask him to tell you what's happened so far. Can he sum up the main characters and events?

Then with the book shut, ask him to tell you about the page or two he's just read.

Has he remembered the important parts of the story? If not, see page 28 for some suggestions.

...AND PREDICTING

Another good way of finding out how well she's understood the story is to ask her to predict what will happen next. What matters here is whether or not the predictions make sense in the light of what's already happened.

FILLING THE GAPS

For this activity you'll need to find a different part of the book you were using before, or a different one altogether. (We've used our story to illustrate this activity.)

Filling in gaps is a technique which is widely used in schools. It involves covering up some of the words in a passage and seeing if your child can guess what they are. Probably the best way to do this is to cover the selected words with small bits of **BLU-TACK** – this won't harm the book. You can cover any words you choose but the way we describe below is well worth a try.

Find a passage of about two hundred words. Leave the first paragraph alone. Then cover every seventh word – you can see the effect on our example. See if your child can guess what the covered words are – and make a note of her guesses. If possible repeat the activity with several different passages from the same book. If you treat this as a game it can be good fun!

Then work out roughly how many your child got correct: count as correct any answer that is either the same as the covered word or an alternative which makes sense.

About 65% (or ⅔) correct or more

This means your child can generally make sense of the text. The book is at an appropriate level.

Between about 40% and 65% correct

This suggests that your child needs some help in understanding this text. Some ways of giving such help are given on page 28.

Less than 40% correct

This means that your child will probably gain little from trying to read this, even with help. This book is almost certainly too difficult. Your child would do better with something more appropriate.

COMPREHENSION QUESTIONS

'*Comprehension*' – reading for meaning and thinking about what you read – *is what reading is all about*. 'Comprehension questions' may bring back memories from when you were at school. We've deliberately left them until last! Questions are a good way of checking children's understanding, but they can sometimes be a bit dreary.

If you want to try asking some questions, read these points carefully. Then you can choose the kinds of questions you want to ask and make up your own. Still treat it as a game – not as a test!

(a) The *easiest* questions can be answered without really understanding the passage at all! If you don't believe that, look at this sentence.

> ❝ *There are two sorts of nurdles – those with girded frolls and those with ungirded frolls.* ❞

What are the two sorts of frolls? You should be able to answer this question without having the slightest idea of what nurdles are, let alone girded and ungirded frolls!

Many comprehension questions are like this. They may get you to read the passage, but you don't really have to take it in. Examples of this kind of question, using our story, would be, 'Which side of the road was the house on?' or, 'Where was the rubbish?' Here, all you need to do is to find the appropriate sentence and copy it out. This is *exactly* what many children have learned to do. Such questions may be more useful if tried from memory rather than with the book open. Asking a couple of easy questions like these may be a good idea to start with.

(b) *Slightly harder* questions involve collecting or re-writing bits of information from the passage. An example, using our story, is, 'How many times did he knock at the front door?'

(c) *More difficult* (and interesting) questions begin to involve the reader in making inferences about what they have read. In other words, the right answer isn't actually written down in the passage – you have to think about it. An example, using our story, is, 'How do we know his suitcase was heavy?'

(d) Finally, the most *searching* questions ask the child to evaluate what he has read, as in this example, 'How successfully do you think the writer describes David's feelings?' Here there are no right or wrong answers, but such questions *do* demand a lot of children. They can be usefully asked about a whole story too. For example, 'Did you enjoy this book? Why?'

REMEMBER

If you want to ask questions:

- Do find a book that your child likes
- Do think about the different sorts of questions you could use
- Do try them with the book open, or from memory
- Don't treat it like a test!

READING

As children get older, schools expect them to learn more independently. Reading is obviously a very important way of finding things out for yourself. Once a child has reached a 'reading age' of about 9 or 10, there's often less emphasis on *teaching* her to read better, but more on *expecting* her to read effectively. ***Busy teachers really have to assume that most children can read effectively for themselves.***

If you have had a go at the reading assessment on pages 22 and 23, you will now have some ideas about the problems your child might be having. These problems might be to do with *reading skills*, or they might be to do with your child's *attitudes* towards reading. (Look at the pages following for more discussion on skills and attitudes.)

HOW CAN *SUCCESS!* HELP?

WHAT'S THE PROBLEM?

If your child is *not very enthusiastic* about reading generally he may actually be tempted by the attractive and entertaining activities in *Success!* It may look as if it's all fun and no work, but if you look at the 'Reading skills' which are covered in Reading Activity book 1 you will see that the thinking behind every activity is very serious indeed!

If your child tends to make *careless errors* when reading aloud, try the activities which concentrate on getting the child to look at individual words.

AN ESSENTIAL TOOL

- If your child shows *little interest* in reading for enjoyment look at the activities which introduce her to some good children's stories.

- If your child seems to find it difficult to *understand or remember* what she reads, there are lots of **Success!** activities which can help.

- If your child has problems *using* what she reads to find out information then there are many activities which are worth trying.

And if your child runs into difficulties, be there to help and encourage. If she is able to do the activities on her own, be ready with your praise.

BUT HOW WILL *SUCCESS!* LINK WITH WHAT MY CHILD DOES AT SCHOOL?

DARTS AT SCHOOL

Many teachers now use techniques known as DARTS – Directed Activities Related to Text – based on the work of Professor Derek Lunzer and Dr Keith Gardner. Some of the pages in the *Success!* Reading Activity and Practice books may just look like fun, but they are in fact based on DARTS activities. The main idea is to encourage children to read in an active way and to get them to think about what they read. Techniques include the following:

Sequencing Children have to rearrange bits of text into the correct order. They aren't put off by having to write, but they certainly have to think about what they read. Sequencing could be particularly important in subjects such as history or science.

Matching This usually involves pairing up pictures or diagrams with text. It is very useful in a range of school subjects, including geography and maths (e.g. shape and area).

Modelling The child has to do something (e.g. draw a picture or make a model) on the basis of what she has read. This again could help in a range of subjects, including CDT (craft-design-technology) or project work.

Predicting Saying what will happen next is a valuable exercise required in subjects as various as English and science.

Cloze These are activities in which the child has to fill in missing words. It is now very widely used across a whole range of school subjects, especially on worksheets.

Questions These are still common too, but instead of being asked traditional comprehension questions, children are encouraged to think about different sorts of questions and to ask themselves questions about what they read. This also helps them with creative writing.

HOW CAN YOU

Your child may not have a positive attitude to reading *because* she has a poor self-image – she sees herself as a poor reader. (You'll find some ideas for helping self-image generally on page 54.)

It's so easy for a vicious circle like this to become established. Not trying can be a *cause* of failure, but it can also be a *result* of failure, and this is very true of reading.

If you feel that your child's attitudes to reading are not all they should be, there are ways that you can help – but don't overdo it!

Do give her praise and encouragement so that she becomes less negative about herself and reading.

Do work with her to improve her actual reading skills and fluency.

As a parent, you know your child better than anybody, and you are probably in a better position than any teacher to improve the way she feels about herself as a reader. If you can give her the encouragement to practise, this will help her develop the skills for herself.

You have more influence over her than any teacher. But make sure that your concern does not backfire and increase her anxiety about reading. Enjoy working together, but remember, **it has to be a co-operative effort, not you telling your child what to do.**

POOR READING SKILLS → POOR READING ATTITUDES → sees self as poor reader → avoids reading → doesn't practise reading skills → reads badly

IMPROVING READING ATTITUDES

These suggestions will encourage your child to see reading as an enjoyable, valuable activity.

SET AN EXAMPLE

Do you read for enjoyment? If not, don't be too hard on your child! If you do, then let him see that reading can be enjoyable.

If you are reading a book at the moment, let your child see you reading it. Talk about it with him. Show him particularly interesting bits.

In a number of schools now there is a short time each day, when everyone in the school, including the head and all the teachers, reads something quietly, just for enjoyment. This is given the impressive name of Uninterrupted Sustained Silent Reading – or USSR for short!

Children learn a lot by example, and that includes reading.

FIND AN INTEREST

If your child has any particular interests, encourage him to read up about them. Your local librarian will be happy to help, and your newsagent should be able to tell you about the hundreds of magazines now available. Many books are based on TV programmes or have programmes based on them. **Try and share your child's interest**, even if you don't feel particularly enthusiastic about the top twenty or BMX bikes! It's no good imposing your interests on your child, however fascinating you think deep sea diving or vegetarian cooking might be! Remember that the magazines may be quite difficult to read and you may need to offer some help. (See the suggestions below on improving reading skills.)

READ A 'CLIFFHANGER'

A technique, which we have used in the Reading Activity books, is to get your child interested in a story, break it off at a really exciting moment and then get him to finish it off for himself.

In the Activity books, we've turned the first few pages of some particularly good children's books into comic strip form to encourage your child to want to read the actual book.

At home, you can read a story aloud up to some suitable 'cliffhanger' and then encourage your child to finish it for himself. Collections of short stories are particularly effective because they are less daunting than a full length story.

If your child is anxious about reading, never expect him to read very much at a time – even a few lines may be enough, but remember it should still be interesting. And don't forget to praise him afterwards.

LISTENING AND READING

If your child tends to read in a flat, monotonous way, he can learn a lot by listening to you read aloud. If you feel your own reading doesn't set a brilliant example, there are many excellent tapes now on the market. You could look together for the ones accompanied by books or magazines, where children can actually follow the story as they listen – if this idea appeals to your child.

OTHER SORTS OF READING

It's worth remembering that reading *isn't* just about stories. We are reading other things every day. Try to involve your child in reading road signs, recipes or instructions, for example. Don't just demand that they read – give the reading some *purpose*.

It doesn't matter what position your child is in – it's enjoying reading that's important!

HELP MORE?

Finally, do note that many of the reading activities mentioned involve not only reading but also other forms of language – speaking, listening, understanding and writing.

Reading is a language skill which shouldn't be seen in isolation.

Boxed games

There are several games like 'Scrabble' now on the market. If your child enjoys playing them, then by all means encourage this, but remember that such games tend to be about individual words rather than reading for meaning. They can help to develop vocabulary and reading skills in a limited way, but they are much more valuable for developing positive reading attitudes.
Other games which may help develop interest in reading are the quiz or mime games, in which players need actually to understand what is written on the card to be successful.

Having fun with reading

1 You can play games with newspapers or magazines. One person opens the magazine and reads a sentence from any article, out loud. The other person then looks at the contents page or headlines and has to guess where the extract came from. If you use a newspaper, limit it to one sheet or spread, though.
If your child is reading sentences for you to find, see whether he can choose 'easy' or 'hard' ones.
This activity helps the child to think about both title and content, encouraging him to make intelligent guesses.

2 A variation of the last game encourages the development of the very useful skill of scanning (see page 29). Play the same game, but this time the person listening has actually to find the chosen sentence. Add a touch of competition by setting a time limit.

3 Scanning is also involved when you look up a telephone number. Why not get your child to help, next time you use the telephone directory? Similar skills are required for looking through a catalogue. Your child could help fill in an order form.

4 Recipes and instructions (for example, for assembling a furniture kit) can involve quite sophisticated reading skills. Recipes have the advantage that you can eat the results. Let your child see whether the instructions are in the right order.

5 Television is often seen as the great enemy of reading. ('Why don't you turn that television off and do something worthwhile, like read a book?') Even television can generate interest in reading.
(a) Books based on TV series are very popular.

(b) Programme details published in the TV magazines and newspapers can be used to encourage a bit of useful reading. 'What's the film about?' (scanning, see page 29); 'What time is it on?' (skimming, see page 29); 'Guess what I'm going to watch tonight!'

(c) It's interesting to compare TV (or film) and printed versions of the same thing. Children may be very surprised to find that a TV version of a book misses some bits out, or adds bits that aren't actually there.

(d) Another interesting game is to listen to the TV or radio news, then see which items are printed in the newspaper. You can try this the other way round – looking at the main newspaper stories and predicting which will be on the TV or radio news, but remember that, by its nature, the TV or radio is the faster medium and can usually get there first.

USING THE ASSESSMENT TECHNIQUES

All the activities we've suggested on pages 22-23 can help you assess how well your child reads and understands. Such activities are not intended to be a one-off assessment. Modern ideas about **assessment** suggest that it **should be part of learning, not separate from it.** So, use the activities like predicting, filling in gaps or answering questions from time to time to help your child think about what he reads.

CONTEXT BUILDING

If your child has problems like those mentioned in 'Reading aloud' on page 22, encourage him to use the *context* of the story to read more fluently.

Look at this sentence:

   Amy turned on the tap and filled the cup with w_ _ _ _ _.

You didn't need to see the last word in order to be able to read the sentence. The context allowed you to guess what the word would be. A glance at the first letter would confirm the most likely guess as 'water' (rather than 'beer' or 'petrol'!).

WHAT YOU CAN DO

Stage 1 Read a sentence or two of a story out loud, then ask your child to read the same bit, again out loud. This will give your child confidence and a model to follow. It also will free her from having to decode every single word, so that she concentrates on the meaning.

Stage 2 As she gets better, increase the amount you read, so that she can't quite remember it word for word!

Stage 3 Now do the same thing, but don't quite finish the sentence, inviting her to do it for herself. Start with just one word left to read, and increase the number gradually – don't do above two or three words at this stage. Accept that your child may still make mistakes.

IMPROVING

Stage 4 Instead of reading the sentence aloud, tell her a bit about it, or ask a question which will give useful clues. Suppose the sentence is:

> *An old wooden sign pointed up the hill.*

If you think she might get stuck on the word 'sign' in particular, you could say, 'Let's see which way the sign pointed.' You've then provided the difficult word as well as giving a general idea of what the sentence is about.

This technique may take a bit of practice, but it again frees your child from some of the anxieties of decoding and gives her a context similar to the one which fluent readers create for themselves.

Reading skills like skimming and scanning become increasingly important as children get older.

READING SKILLS

NOT THAT STORY AGAIN!

Don't try to prevent your child from re-reading the same story again. Re-reading a familiar story has two advantages.

1 It's reassuring and helps the child feel less anxious about reading, so it helps reading *attitudes*.

2 It gives a familar context for the child to practise reading fluently, so it helps reading *skills*.

Many adults choose to read 'easy' books for relaxation and pleasure so don't be critical of your child doing the same thing!

PAIRED READING

Some research has shown this technique to be very effective. Here, you read, not before the child, but actually at the same time and at the speed set by the child. When your child feels confident enough to read alone, he gives a signal, like a tap on the table, and then you stop. A repeat of the signal means the child wants you to start reading along again.

The big advantage of this technique is that the pace and the amount of support are decided by the child. It is not so much the technique that is important but the parent's interest and involvement.

SKIMMING AND SCANNING

Good reading doesn't stop once a child can read accurately and fluently. As children get older they need to use their reading for many different school subjects. Reading skills like skimming and scanning become increasingly important.

Skimming is glancing quickly through the text to get a general idea of what it's all about. This is useful, but is quite a difficult skill to master.

Scanning is probably easier to develop. Here, you again look quickly through the text without reading every word, but your aim is to find a specific word or point of information.

A range of useful study skills appear in the *Success!* Practice book 'Reading for Facts'.

CHANGING ROLES

Why not let your child get his own back and use some of these techniques in reverse!

The story so far If you've both read the same book or passage, you can summarise it for him. You could make some deliberate mistakes to see if he spots them!

Filling the gaps He can choose the blanks for you to fill in. This is a very useful exercise if you stipulate, for example, 'hard' words or 'gaps where there's only one answer'. In choosing the words, he will have to think carefully about meaning.

Comprehension questions Let him ask you the questions. This is very useful if you can discuss the different kinds of questions.

Ask him to think of a question where the answer is obvious. Or another question where it's a matter of opinion.

Trying the techniques in reverse will help your child in two ways:

1 Without realising it, he will be practising reading and thinking carefully about what he reads, thus improving his reading *skills*.

2 It will change the activities from being a 'test' to something you can enjoy sharing. Children will enjoy getting their own back!

How well does

PRESENTATION

Children in school spend a lot of time doing written work. As they get older it becomes increasingly important that **they should be able to to write neatly, accurately, quickly and in an interesting way.**

On this page the focus is on the *neatness* of your child's work – her handwriting.

This assessment is based on one small sample. To build up a full picture, check other examples of her normal handwriting.

WHAT TO DO

Here are the two extracts. Ask your child to choose the one he likes better.

Explain to your child that you're interested in seeing how *neatly* he can write. *Ask him to choose one of the extracts and copy it out in his best handwriting, on lined paper.* Wide feint lines are best.

Don't watch him do it! Go out of the room and say you'll come back in five minutes. Your child won't do his best if you're peering over his shoulder. Five minutes should give ample time.

When you return, praise his efforts. *Don't criticise*, even if you can spot mistakes or if you think it isn't very neat.

HOW TO ASSESS YOUR CHILD'S HANDWRITING

Later, when your child is busy doing something else, look carefully at what he's written.

This *should* be a sample of your child's best handwriting. Each passage contains every letter of the alphabet at least once, so you can look at how your child has formed each letter.

Here are some points to look out for:

▶ Look for inappropriate capital letters – a common mistake.

▶ Does the writing lean consistently in the same direction? A larger sample would help to assess this, but variations in this or letter consistency suggest that your child hasn't yet decided on a handwriting style of his own.

▶ Are the letters even? For example, 'a' and 'r' should be the same height, while 'g' and 'y' should be the same length below the line.

Wendy just gazed at the mysterious black box. She felt very excited.
She knew she shouldn't have taken the key, but she didn't care if she got into trouble now. She turned the key quietly in the lock and opened the lid.

OR

Jack was getting quite scared. If the balloons burst he'd fall.
The zoo was far below him now, and all that money was just extra weight. His arms were beginning to ache. And then, above his head, he heard it – a gentle hissing sound.

▶ Are the letters actually on the line? Sometimes children may write a 'y', for example, so that the whole letter is on the line, rather than with the tail coming below it.

▶ Are the letters excessively big or small? Huge letters can mean that your child is having problems forming and controlling the writing, while tiny ones can indicate a lack of confidence. Don't read too much into this. Discuss any worries you may have with your child's teacher.

▶ Are there any problems with joining up letters? Joined up handwriting is much quicker to do than printing each letter separately, but some children find it difficult at first. If you suspect problems, this is one area where it helps actually to *watch* your child write and look for hesitations or awkwardness.

▶ Is the spacing between the words reasonable? Look in particular for words running into each other without spaces. This suggests inability to plan ahead.

▶ Has your child accurately predicted how much space a word will need? Look for words squashed into the end of the line to fit, or words frequently being split between one line and the next.

▶ Finally, and *most important*, is it *legible*? See if somebody else can read isolated words, with the rest covered up! Check after a week or so to see if your child can read his own writing!

your child write?

READABILITY

Now look at a piece of your child's writing to assess accuracy (spelling and punctuation) and content, as well as neatness (handwriting).

WHAT TO DO

Talk to your child about what she would like to write about. It must be something which really interests her. It could be a story from her favourite TV programme – or part of a longer story which she knows very well. If she likes the idea she might choose to finish off the story which she chose to copy (see opposite page).

If she wants to discuss it with you first, that's fine, but try to draw out her ideas rather than impose yours. When your child is ready to start, go out of the room again but don't fix a time limit on your return this time. Don't say anything about 'best handwriting' – if she asks just tell her to do it in her 'normal writing'.

When she's finished, read and praise her efforts again, picking out any specific good points you notice.

Finally, ask if she thinks there are any mistakes in what she's written, and help to correct them if she wants you to.

ASSESSING YOUR CHILD'S WRITING

NEATNESS

Compare the handwriting she did before with what she's done now. Use the list of points about handwriting on the opposite page. If possible, compare other samples of 'best' and 'normal' or 'rough' handwriting. Don't worry if there are differences – there should be!

ACCURACY

Accuracy refers to spelling and punctuation. The box on the right contains an example of a child's writing – it is a continuation of one of our story openings. It illustrates the points to look for.

Spelling

1 First, was your child able to spot any mistakes for herself? This is an encouraging sign and suggests careless slips rather than inability to spell. Do note if your child has indicated any 'errors' which were in fact correct. This could mean uncertainty about spelling or a lack of confidence in her own ability to spell. As with reading, both skills and attitudes could be involved.

2 Although incorrect, these do sound right. Check to see if there are other mistakes like this, or if they are isolated examples. If such errors are common, your child is relying on the *sound* of the word to guess at its spelling. See page 35 for help.

3 and **4** These suggest uncertainties about how to add 'ed' to make the past tense. Again, you'd need to check if these errors are frequent to see if they are signs of poor understanding or careless slips.

5 Here the child has actually written a 'b' instead of a 'd'. This is called a *reversal*. Such reversals are very common among young children, but it can persist in some older ones.

Punctuation and grammar

6 This is a very common mistake which you can see repeated on many market stalls! Your child may be uncertain about what plurals are and how they differ from an 's' added to a word to show possession.

7 This shows a lack of awareness of what sentences are – a common, basic source of problems. Get your child to read it aloud to you and see if he pauses in the proper places. See page 35 for further help.

8 Rather more difficult, but still common – a lack of proper punctuation when writing direct speech. Many children find this particularly difficult. You can turn to page 35 for some ideas on how to help.

CONTENT

This is notoriously difficult to assess. What one person thinks is rubbish, another may think is wonderful! However, think about these aspects.

Length

The child who wrote the example was clearly not inspired by our story! Was what your child wrote as brief? Writing very little can be a result of anxiety. It can also be because the child finds writing very laborious. We do tend to underestimate the physical difficulties of writing. A child may have enough ideas to fill a novel but may give up after writing 10 lines. If you think this could be her problem, ask your child to *tell* you what she could have written.

Development of ideas

Note how this child hasn't used what was available. There's no mention of the zoo or the money. The ideas aren't developed at all. How did your child do?

Style

In our example, note how it's all action. One event quickly follows another. There's no description of the scene or of people, their thoughts or feelings. This is a very common style among children of this age group. It may suggest a lack of involvement with the task. Help your child by talking or asking questions like, 'How did he feel? What did it look like?'

Sense of audience

Your child has done this piece of writing for you. It is important that you give her your opinion of it – but remember to emphasise the positive. See page 37 for advice on being the audience for your child's writing.

Ask your child what *she* thought of it. Did she enjoy writing it? Did she find it interesting but hard to continue? There are some useful points about 'Getting them to write' on page 37.

---

① Then a plain ② came up and it fird ③ its gun's ⑥ at him and shot him ⑤ bown ⑦ he ⑧ landed in the sea ⑦ he shouted help help but it was to ② late and he drownd ④ the end

Writing is H·A·R·D WORK

HOW CAN *SUCCESS!* HELP?

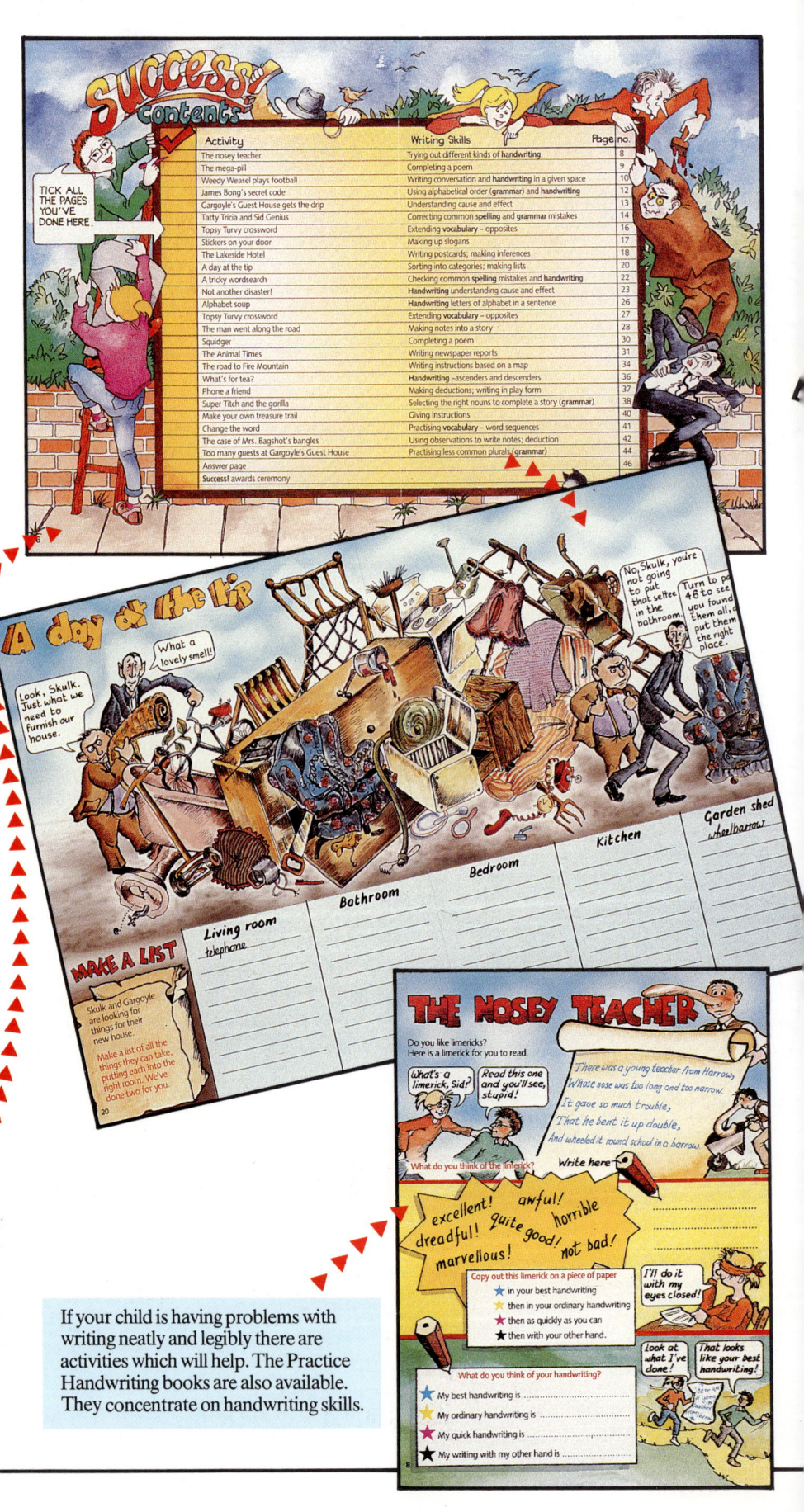

Your child's writing problems may involve either *skills* or *attitudes* or both. To write successfully we need *adequate skills* and *positive attitudes*. The two are very closely linked, as with reading (see pages 26 and 27). There are also two other important ingredients:

A purpose – few of us are likely to write just for the enjoyment of writing.

An audience – who is the writing for?

It is the purpose and the audience which will decide what sort of writing is needed.

When we as adults ask children to write something, we may be expecting them to do some or all of these things at the same time, depending on the purpose and the audience:
- write neatly (not just legibly)
- write quickly, or at least produce quite a lot in a given time
- write accurately, with no spelling or grammatical mistakes
- write interestingly or creatively, communicating something worthwhile, or at least true

When you think about it, that's very demanding! When was the last time you wrote something which met all those demands? Is it surprising that many children are not very keen on writing, even when they can write reasonably well?

If your child is not very keen on writing he may well be motivated by the colourful and fun activities in **Success!** Don't be misled into thinking that it's all fun and no work. If you look at the 'Writing skills' which are covered in Writing Activity book 1 you can see that the intention behind every activity is very serious indeed!

If your child is having problems with writing neatly and legibly there are activities which will help. The Practice Handwriting books are also available. They concentrate on handwriting skills.

Activity	Writing Skills	Page no.
The nosey teacher	Trying out different kinds of handwriting	8
The mega-pill	Completing a poem	9
Weedy Weasel plays football	Writing conversation and handwriting in a given space	10
James Bong's secret code	Using alphabetical order (grammar) and handwriting	12
Gargoyle's Guest House gets the drip	Understanding cause and effect	13
Tatty Tricia and Sid Genius	Correcting common spelling and grammar mistakes	14
Topsy Turvy crossword	Extending vocabulary – opposites	16
Stickers on your door	Making up slogans	17
The Lakeside Hotel	Writing postcards; making inferences	18
A day at the tip	Sorting into categories; making lists	20
A tricky wordsearch	Checking common spelling mistakes and handwriting	22
Not another disaster!	Handwriting understanding cause and effect	23
Alphabet soup	Handwriting letters of alphabet in a sentence	26
Topsy Turvy crossword	Extending vocabulary – opposites	27
The man went along the road	Making notes into a story	28
Squidger	Completing a poem	30
The Animal Times	Writing newspaper reports	31
The road to Fire Mountain	Writing instructions based on a map	34
What's for tea?	Handwriting – ascenders and descenders	36
Phone a friend	Making deductions; writing in play form	37
Super Titch and the gorilla	Selecting the right nouns to complete a story (grammar)	38
Make your own treasure trail	Giving instructions	40
Change the word	Practising vocabulary – word sequences	41
The case of Mrs. Bagshot's bangles	Using observations to write notes; deduction	42
Too many guests at Gargoyle's Guest House	Practising less common plurals (grammar)	44
Answer page		46
Success! awards ceremony		

If spelling is a problem, there are ways to tackle some common mistakes. Practice Spelling books will help your child to improve his spelling.

If it's accuracy in terms of grammar and punctuation that is a problem, look for the *Success!* activities which encourage an awareness of how words function and the way punctuation works.

If motivation is needed, *Success!* Writing books outline a whole range of stimulating and funny purposes for writing. See, too, the Practice book on 'Writing Letters'.

If your child's imagination requires stimulating try the creative writing activities.

BUT HOW WILL *SUCCESS!* LINK WITH WHAT MY CHILD DOES AT SCHOOL?

School work means a great deal of writing, but as we've seen, writing involves complex skills. The *Success!* writing activities are as challenging as school work but we've set out to motivate your child by providing livelier and more humorous reasons for writing. They also cover all the basic skills of writing, namely handwriting, spelling, vocabulary, grammar and punctuation.

We all like to see neat handwriting but teachers will tell you that too much emphasis on neatness can, in fact, be damaging. In the *Success!* series, as in school, we maintain that children's writing should always be legible to the person it was meant for, and that children should be able to write neatly when appropriate. Because different schools use different sorts of handwriting, we deliberately do not ask your child to copy one style as a model – instead she is asked to use the style she is used to.

While teachers think that spelling is very important, most would agree that helping your child learn how to spell is what matters most. Teachers would agree also that children are more likely to extend their vocabulary if they find words *fun*.

Grammar is always a controversial subject! What *Success!* does is to encourage children to think about how words work together, and about how proper punctuation is vital for communicating meaning. You will find words like 'adverb' and 'noun' but they are introduced in a very gentle way so that nobody can get alarmed!

It is writing for communication which matters most at school, as it matters most in adult life. It's no use being able to write, spell and punctuate beautifully if you have nothing to say! The *Success!* activities involve your child in many types of writing, all of which are important at school, e.g. stories, letters, charts, notes, reports, lists, poems.

And as for providing an audience for your child's writing – well, that's up to you!

What can you do about

NEATNESS

HANDWRITING

We don't want to over-emphasise the importance of neat handwriting but it is important in two ways.

(a) Writing must always be *legible enough for the intended reader* (even if it's only for yourself).
(b) Children should be able to write neatly *when neatness is appropriate* (e.g. on a notice or an invitation).

1 Children really do need encouragement about their handwriting.

2 It is helpful sometimes to watch *how* your child writes, especially if there are problems with particular letters. Your child may be forming the letter badly, especially by beginning in the wrong place.

> *My eldest son used to draw the dot on the 'i' before the rest of the letter!*

It may be hard for your child to break the habit but it's worth trying if it's obviously causing problems to him or for the reader.

3 Handwriting problems can actually be a *result* of other writing problems. For example:

> *One girl would scribble difficult words in the hope that she could disguise her spelling problems.*

There is research which suggests that poor handwriting and poor spelling are very closely linked.

4 Check your child's posture. How does he sit when he writes? What about the angle of the paper? You'll find tips on these things in the **Success!** Practice Handwriting books.

5 Check how your child is holding the pen or pencil. Too tight a grip (which may suggest anxiety) can cause problems. Pressing too hard is a related fault. If your child is left-handed you might want to look at 'Lefthanders at school'.

6 Do you have access to a typewriter or a wordprocessor? These can be helpful to children who are anxious about their handwriting. It's very encouraging to see your work beautifully set out for once!

7 How can you tell when your child is trying to write as neatly as possible? One way which teachers use is to look at the first piece of school work done in a new exercise book or for a new teacher. Almost all children will produce their best handwriting under such circumstances.

Children should be encouraged to take a real pride in the appearance of their written work.

ACCURACY

SPELLING

Encouraging your child to read more may help with spelling, but for many children it isn't enough. What they need are *strategies* for improving their spelling. We suggest such strategies in the **Success!** Practice Spelling books.

One strategy is particularly effective. Most adults have problems spelling certain words. Try Study, Cover, Write, Check yourself and see how it works!

Study Cover
Write Check

Study *Look* carefully at the word, particularly at any bits you think you might get wrong. Shut your eyes and try to imagine the word written down.
  say the letters out loud to yourself
  write the word with your finger, making the movements carefully
Cover the word up so that you can't see it.
Write it down. *Don't* copy it. Try to remember it by thinking how it *looked*, how the letters *sounded* and how your hand *moved* to write it.
Check if you got it right. If you didn't, *look* again at the bit you got wrong in particular. Shut your eyes and imagine the word with these letters written extra large, or in a different colour. Then *say* the letters again, pronouncing the ones you got wrong extra loudly. Now *write* the word, making the wrong letters extra big. Practise the word a few more times over the next few weeks so that you don't forget it.

OTHER THINGS YOU CAN DO

✳ Try deliberate mispronunciation. It's fun too! This works best for words which are very familiar to the child (so she knows they aren't really pronounced like that!). It's also good for 'silent' letters, which may be missed out because they aren't sounded e.g. 'ker-nife' instead of 'knife'.

✳ Mnemonics are useful too. The trick is to think of a sentence with the words beginning with the letters you need to remember. For example, children often mis-spell 'Wednesday' but won't if they remember the mnemonic:

We Eat Dry Noodles Every Suppertime On Wednesdays

Children can enjoy making these up, although they can be quite hard to do. See page 11 for how to use mnemonics to improve the memory.

✳ Encourage your child to keep a book of words he's learning to spell. It is much better to concentrate on the words your child wants to learn rather than giving him lists of words which you think he should learn.

✳ Do remember that English spelling isn't easy. There are rules but they're often complicated and have many exceptions. If you learnt spelling through rules just think how many you still use – probably only one or two! This is why they aren't used in **Success!**

✳ Using a dictionary is a good way of checking a spelling but you may need to be able to spell the word first in order to find it!

neatness and accuracy?

Practising pauses

1 (a) Read a story aloud to your child slowly, with all the pauses. Ask him to raise his hand whenever he notices a pause.
(b) Ask him to recite something he knows by heart, without reading, so that you can indicate the pauses.
(c) Now do the same two things again, agreeing on different signals for long pauses (full stops) and short pauses (commas). Be prepared for your child to find this quite difficult.
(d) Alternatively, you could do this together while listening to a tape.

This isn't so easy as the pauses may not always be obvious and the speed will be greater – and your child may copy your signals! But it will help him become more aware of the pauses.

2 Show your child how pauses are indicated in writing. Some children may not even notice the punctuation, particularly if they are not very fluent readers and are concentrating on the letters and words rather than the meaning. Find an old comic, book or magazine. Go over all the commas and full stops in felt tip, making them extra big and using two different colours. Now read it together slowly, pausing appropriately.

A boy once wrote:

yrntn

What do you think he was trying to write?
(Answer at the bottom of the page.)

This is an extreme example, but many children spell words the way they sound rather than according to the arbitrary way they're spelt. For example, 'freight' could be spelt frait, frate, phrait, phrate or phreight – they all sound right. If your child does this don't tell him he's stupid – agree that the word could be spelt like that, but say that it just isn't. In other words, it's not his fault, it's the world's!

PUNCTUATION

Full stops and commas
If your assessment showed that your child is having problems with punctuation, it's a good idea to get her to read aloud what she wrote, to see if she pauses appropriately at where commas or full stops should be, even if she missed them out. If she doesn't pause appropriately, see if you can make her aware of the existence of pauses, by doing the first game in the 'Practising pauses' box.

If she does pause appropriately, talk about why it sounds better with the pauses and how commas, full stops and the break between paragraphs indicate progressively longer pauses. (Don't worry about colons and semi-colons at this stage.) Try the second game in the 'Practising pauses' box.

Punctuating speech
You could try the second 'Practising pauses' game for getting your child to notice how speech is punctuated with inverted commas – a problem for many children.

Your child might also enjoy re-writing cartoons in comics into ordinary speech – this method is used in the **Success!** Activity books.

Apostrophes

Another common punctuation problem is not missing something out but putting it where it's not needed! It's the problem of apostrophes, and lots of adults have problems with them too! On many a market stall or shop window can be seen examples like these:

Video's for hire
pork chop's
Granny Smiths apple's

These are the rules – just to remind you!

You don't need an apostrophe for a plural word – chops, videos, tomatoes.
You do need an apostrophe *before* a letter 's' when:
● there's a letter or letters missed out – *what's* instead of *what is*
● when something belongs to somebody – Granny Smith's apples
You do need an apostrophe *after* the letter 's' when
● something belongs to more than one person – The footballers' shirts.

Left-handers at school

Being left-handed does not automatically lead to problems with handwriting, sport or anything else.

Are you sure your child is left-handed?

Some children have no strong preference – they may do some tasks with the left hand and some with the right. (Watch how your child draws, picks up a small object, etc.) If this is true of your child you may be able to encourage him to use his right hand rather than his left.

If your child always uses his left hand, don't force him to become right-handed.

Do make sure the teacher knows your child is left-handed so that she can provide left-handed scissors, hockey sticks, etc.
Do check that when your child is sitting with another child, he is on the left, so that his left hand is free.
Do give your child extra help in mastering skills which involve right and left; these include reading and writing.
Do make sure that when he is writing, your child's paper is tilted up to the left, not to the right.
Do check his grip on the pen. It should be normal, but slightly higher up so that he can see what he has just written. The 'claw' grip, where the hand curls round the pen awkwardly should be discouraged, unless it's really well-established.

Answer wire netting

WHAT CAN YOU DO ABOUT CONTENT?

How can we help children write neatly, quickly, accurately *and* interestingly all at the same time?

When we look at a child's writing, it's easier to concentrate on handwriting or spelling and punctuation than on what the child is actually saying! The trouble is that the content is not so obviously wrong or right, so it's harder to improve.

DRAFTING AND REDRAFTING

This is a way that is recognised by many teachers. It is used as a basis for some of the *Success!* activities. There's an example in the box. Here the child is finishing one of the stories on page 30. This is what you do:

1 Your child needs an exercise book or folder with both left-hand and right-hand pages. On the left-hand page he can write anything he likes! He can use notes or pictures, try out different spellings and different ideas. Of course this is exactly what many professional writers do. The right hand page is for the final, neat version.

2 Talk about what your child is going to write about. It will mean more to him if he's writing something he's got to do for school anyway, or if it has a purpose of its own.

3 Explain the difference between the left 'rough' page and the right 'neat' page and encourage him to make a start. Making a start is often the hardest bit! Let's take the example of finishing off the first story on page 30. One way to get your child started is to ask questions like:

- **What** is in the box?
- **Who** put it there?
- **Why** is it locked up?
- **How** does Wendy feel?
- **What** will she do next?

Get your child to write down possible answers, in rough.

You can ask similar questions at later stages if your child has indicated that he needs help in deciding what to put next.

4 As he writes a rough version, he can indicate any words he's not sure how to spell by underlining them in pencil. Similarly he can indicate where he should like help on other things. You could, for example, agree on a sign which he can insert wherever he needs help with what else to put. It doesn't matter how messy it is!

5 When he's ready, see where he is asking for your help. Talk it through and encourage him to make a second draft if necessary before trying to do a final version.

6 This method has several advantages: your child *asks* you for help, you don't intervene until requested; your child needn't feel so anxious about mistakes.

DOING PROJECTS

The drafting and redrafting technique lends itself to other forms of writing as well.

Project work is increasingly common in schools. Any teacher will tell you that **many children simply copy out chunks from books, often without really understanding them.** This is avoided if your child makes notes on the rough left hand page, preferably using more than one source of information, and then writes up the final version from the rough one, without looking at the books.

---

underlining used to show child isn't sure of spelling

spelling corrected by you

additional bit put in after discussion with you

sign to indicate he needs help with what else to put

ignore the doodles and blots

36

NOTE-TAKING

As children get older they are expected to work independently more and more. Note-taking is a key skill here, which many children find very difficult. Here are some ideas to help.

Copying out chunks of text is fine, in moderation, but some children need help in pruning the text into manageable pieces.

Abbreviations are useful. Here is a list of common ones, and some adaptations.

∴	therefore
∵	because
/	the
→	caused or led to
↛	did not cause or lead to
>	greater or bigger than
<	smaller or less than
=	is equal to, or the same as
≠	is not equal to or the same as
⚡	problem or conflict

No doubt you can add to the list.

Working from notes If your child is working on a project, encourage him to work from notes rather than from the book directly.

Colour coding If your child has to learn what is in her own notes, encourage her to write important words in different colours and to use sketches and doodles. Making notes more visual helps to make them memorable.

Diagrams Try using diagrams, with the main topic in the middle and ideas related to it around the outside.

Outlines Notes can also form the basis for your child's own creative writing (see page 36).

GETTING THEM TO WRITE

WHY WRITE?

Some children will enjoy writing stories for their own sake. If your child does this, give masses of encouragement!

Often, children find it easier to write if there is a *purpose* to doing so. The best way is to encourage them to use writing in 'real-life' situations and about things they are really interested in.

- Do they have a hobby or interest which could provide a reason for writing? (Maybe a letter to the local football club?)
- What about a scrapbook or diary? You could provide the necessary encouragement by providing the scrapbook!
- A special occasion, such as a birthday, can provide lots of reasons for writing – shopping lists, invitations, thank-you letters.

WHO IS IT FOR?

Children also need an audience for their writing if it's to become more than an artificial task. The audience may be themselves (if it's a diary), a friend or a relative (as with a letter) or, of course, you!

Older children who are not normally keen to write have produced some splendid results when they were asked to write for much younger children. Here, at last, was somebody to write for who couldn't read or write as well as they could and who wouldn't laugh at their attempts. So enlist the help of younger brothers, sisters, cousins and friends' children.

If you are the audience for something your child writes *never* let your first comment be critical. **Read it aloud, with lots of expression,** surreptitiously correcting minor errors of expression and ignoring the awful spelling – **give it all you've got!**

> *I remember putting on such a performance of a few lines written by a 'slow learner', only to be asked by the incredulous boy, 'Did I write that?'*

Only after lots of enthusiastic comment should you ask if there's anything they'd like your help with to put right.

LANGUAGE GAMES

Writing is only one form of language which children need to develop. Writing and reading are obviously closely linked, but there are also speaking and listening which we tend to forget as language skills. You may of course feel that your child is already very good at talking and perhaps not so good at listening! Here are some ideas for games you can try with your child which will encourage a positive attitude, not only towards writing, but towards language in general.

✱ Language games, like 'Scrabble', will help your child to develop vocabulary and improve spelling as well as showing that words can be fun. Crosswords and wordsearches can do the same.

✱ You can make up word games yourself quite easily and encourage your child to make them up for you. It's harder than it looks to make up crosswords or wordsearches, but quite easy to make up anagrams or play 'Hangman'.

✱ Try dictionary quizzes. These can involve using phrases and sentences as well as individual words, and also practise valuable 'looking up' study skills. You could ask questions like, 'What does mercenary mean?' or more funny ones like 'If you had a toupée would you eat it, wear it or keep it as a pet?' Give your child the chance to ask *you* such questions too! Wrong answers (deliberate or not) can provide much amusement.

✱ The old party favourite of 'Consequences' involves writing sentences and phrases.

✱ Develop general language skills, at no expense! Two very similar pictures from a puzzle magazine can be used by two players, each of whom sees only one picture. They then have to find the differences, either by asking each other questions or by describing their own picture to the other person. (This is quite difficult! For best results, use 'easy' pairs of pictures.)

✱ For hilarious results, one player draws a simple pattern or picture, then describes it so that the other person can draw it. You can use names of shapes ('Draw a triangle with a square on the top') but not names of things ('Draw a house with a tree on the left'). Comparing the two pictures is not only good fun, it also shows the importance of careful description.

Dyslexia

Dyslexia is a controversial issue. Some academics and some Local Education Authorities don't even recognise the term.

Children (usually boys) who are considered dyslexic are often highly intelligent. Two of the greatest thinkers in history, Leonardo da Vinci and Albert Einstein, are both said to have been dyslexic. However, dyslexics can exhibit a wide range of 'symptoms', including any of the following:

- a clumsiness or delayed language development when young
- a mixture of right and left-handedness (e.g. throwing with the right hand, drawing with the left)
- reversals of letters (e.g. confusing 'b' and 'd') and even mirror writing
- spelling problems – letters in the wrong place or bizarre mis-spellings
- difficulties in telling left from right

This wide range of problems means there's no such thing as a dyslexic 'type' and you should not assume your child is dyslexic because he has some of the above symptoms.

If you want to know more about dyslexia there are addresses on page 71. It is important, if you are worried, to consult an expert.

MATHEMATICS FOR LIFE

> 'Mathematics has a crucial role to play in equipping young people to meet the responsibilities of adult life – as citizens, employees and members of households. At home, for example, we use mathematics daily – in managing the family budget, in comparing price and quantity of goods in the shops, in assessing the real cost of hire purchase agreements and of insurance policies, in measuring up for carpets and curtains and in working out a car's consumption of petrol. As citizens we need to make sense of a growing volume of statistical information, for example about the country's economic position, crime rates, house prices, and trends in average earnings.'
>
> Mathematics National Curriculum Working Group Report 1988

It is easy to think of maths as something which is isolated to the classroom, as something to do with 'sets' and 'decimals', 'algebra', 'area' and 'geometry' and other such terms. **Yet maths is part and parcel of our daily lives – just as much as reading is.** Why not make a quick list of all the things you've done in the last couple of days which involved some kind of mathematical thinking? Did you do any of these, for example?

Check that you had enough cash to do the shopping.
Put change aside for next week's dinner money.
Estimate how much petrol you needed to fill the tank.
Work out how much material you would need for the new curtains.
Decide what size of weedkiller container you would need to deal with weeds on the path.
Pay the milkman.
Weigh the ingredients for a cake.
Work out how much wood you would need for the new bookshelves.
Decide on the time you had to leave to be at the dentist's in time for your appointment.

If your child is having problems with his maths, help him see the point of the calculations he is battling with. One of the most important ways in which you can help is by discussing the real life maths that you have been doing. And be prepared to *listen* to what your child says.

MATHEMATICS IN SCHOOLS TODAY

Many parents feel out of their depth with the way maths is taught today. 'New maths' makes us feel unable to help our children effectively because we were taught to do it differently when we were at school. Some things, indeed, have changed – others have not.

Basic arithmetical skills

These are still the most important thing. It is essential that children should learn the *arithmetical operations*, should be able to recall *number bonds* instantly, should know their *multiplication tables* up to times 10.

What are the operations? This is just a general term for add, subtract, multiply and divide.

School maths is no longer a matter of doing pages of sums.

What are number bonds? These are simple number combinations, for example, the number bonds for 10 are:

$0 + 10$ $7 + 3$
$1 + 9$ $8 + 2$
$2 + 8$ $9 + 1$
$3 + 7$ $10 + 0$
$4 + 6$
$5 + 5$
$6 + 4$

It is as important that children should be able to recall these number bonds instantly as it is that they should know their multiplication tables.

What has changed is that **teachers no longer expect children to learn these basic skills by doing pages of written 'sums'.** Much more emphasis is placed on using these skills within real life contexts.

Mental arithmetic

This is coming back into fashion and is regarded as increasingly important.

> ❝ Using one's head requires a degree of thought and intelligence, so that mental calculation can help to develop understanding as well as simply being quicker in many circumstances. ❞
>
> Mathematics National Curriculum Working Group Report 1988

Understanding maths

There is an increasing emphasis now on ensuring that children understand what they are doing. Understanding is vital if the facts are to be applied to real life.

When anyone learns a new fact, it is easier to absorb and remember if it can be linked with something we already know. The chart on page 42 shows how basic mathematical concepts are all connected.

Estimating the answer

One of the reasons maths has the awesome reputation it has is because we think we must get the right answer. In fact, *in real life maths we hardly ever need to calculate an exact answer.* If you made a list of the mathematical calculations you have done recently, how many of them really needed a precise answer? Most of the time we need an estimate, to know what is 'about right'.

In a world of microcomputers and calculators, being able to estimate becomes increasingly important – we need to be able to estimate the answer to know if we have pressed the wrong key.

The importance of decimals

You may remember 'doing decimals' at school – they may well have seemed rather remote from real life. Our children are surrounded by decimals.

Problem-solving

In everyday situations we often need to use a range of maths skills to solve particular problems. Schools are increasingly using a problem-solving approach to teach maths, so that children can use their maths skills with flexibility and intelligence. You can read more about this aspect of modern education on pages 12 to 16.

The place of the calculator

A lot of people are suspicious about the emphasis that is put on using the calculator in schools today. They feel that children who can get the right answer at the push of a button will not understand the calculations they are doing – and that without a calculator in their hands they will be helpless. They feel that it is only by using pencil and paper that the basic arithmetical skills can really be learnt.

It's an understandable reaction, but calculators, like computers and other aspects of our increasingly technological society, are here to stay. The National Curriculum Working Group has this to say:

> ❝ *It is essential that all pupils leave school knowing how to use a calculator effectively. Using a calculator successfully depends on an understanding of the number operations to be performed ... an estimate of the expected answer, a correct sequence of operations on the keyboard and an intelligent interpretation of the results ... There is evidence that* **using a calculator can help children develop their feel for and understanding of number.** ❞

DEVELOPING A FEEL FOR NUMBER

This has to be the starting point – learning to see numbers as friends to be used in all kinds of interesting and enjoyable ways, rather than as enemies which have somehow to be got under control. You may find it difficult to know whether your child has a feel for number – but there are things you can notice.

? Can your child readily tell you how much change you should get from a pound?
? Can she quickly find a particular page in a book?
? Can he tell you how many plates you'll need when there are visitors?

> Jonathan, at the age of four, lived with mum, dad, a big sister, a little brother and an even littler sister. He was helping to lay the table for Sunday tea when both grannies were visiting, but couldn't count past six. Undaunted, he laid out the plates for the usual number, then went back for one for Nan, and then one for Gran.

ATTITUDES ABOUT MATHS

As has already been said in regard to reading and writing, skills and attitudes are closely linked. If your child is finding maths difficult he's likely to dislike it – if he enjoys maths lessons he's probably mastering the basic skills. Our attitudes to a subject are very important. *If you see maths as interesting and useful, the chances are that your child will regard it in the same way.*

Unfortunately, many grown ups do not feel so positive about maths. 'Will you help me with my reading?' Such a request from your child is likely to have you responding by sitting comfortably with your child on the settee, both of you enjoying the chance to be relaxed and intimate.

'Will you help me with my maths?' Is much more likely to provoke the alarmed reaction, 'You had better go and ask your father!'

In all the *Success!* books the emphasis is on motivating children through getting them to enjoy what they are doing. Nowhere is this more important than in maths.

HOW CAN *SUCCESS!* HELP YOUR CHILD?

The *Success!* Maths Activity books may surprise you. They certainly don't look like the maths books you may be used to. The emphasis is on fun. The books will help your child to be more relaxed about maths and will lessen the anxiety which is so common where this subject is concerned. The activities will also:

Help your child to see that there are different ways of arriving at an answer,
Encourage the careful use of the calculator,
Enable your child to use the important mathematical ideas of order, comparison, investigation, judgement and logical deduction in everyday life.

If you look at the 'Maths skills' which are covered in Maths Activity book 1 you can see that there is a very serious intention behind every activity.

This activity, for example, helps to explain the structure of our numbering system, and shows the fundamental importance of 'ten'. It takes many children a long time to grasp this idea.

MATHEMATICS
— CAN BE ENJOYED

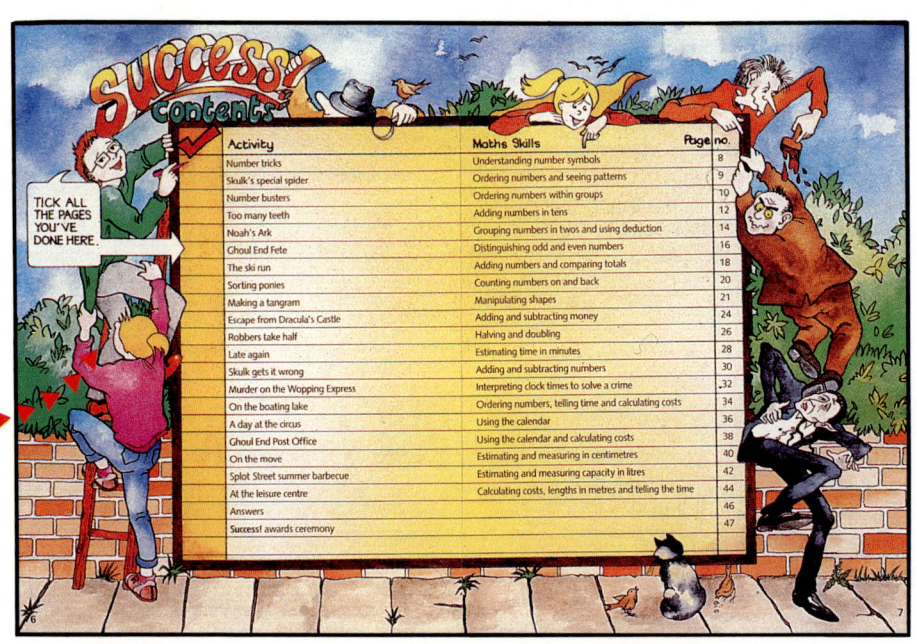

Your child may need help in getting a feel for numbers. There are many activities which concentrate on building confidence in handling numbers.

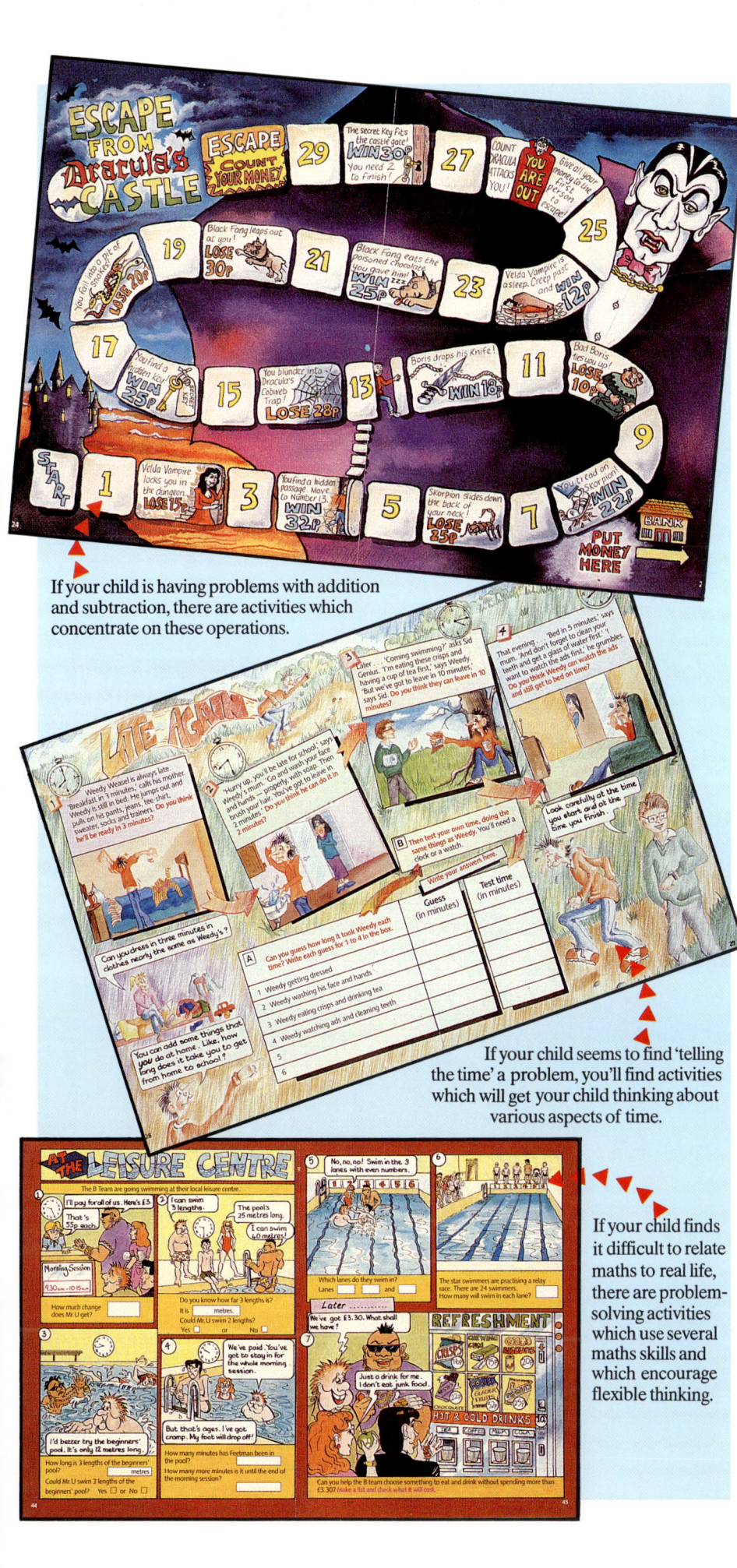

If your child is having problems with addition and subtraction, there are activities which concentrate on these operations.

If your child seems to find 'telling the time' a problem, you'll find activities which will get your child thinking about various aspects of time.

If your child finds it difficult to relate maths to real life, there are problem-solving activities which use several maths skills and which encourage flexible thinking.

All the activities emphasise the place of maths in real life and all set out to motivate your child – maths can really be fun!

What to do about maths phobia

Some children panic over maths. The panic is just as real as, say, an attack of vertigo or a fear of spiders. It can totally prevent new learning or, at least, make progress painful and slow.

If your child panics about maths, working with the *Success!* books and talking about maths will do little to help. Learning in maths builds on what has gone before. If your child has not understood the basic concepts (and there are many reasons why this can happen) it's difficult to make progress.

In this situation it's important that your child talks to someone she trusts. This may be the class teacher or another professional.

As her parent, don't let your child think she is stupid – do what you can to help her build up her self-image (see pages 52-54). Once your child is making progress then the *Success!* books can play their part.

WHAT YOU CAN DO TO HELP

REMEMBER

- **Do** concentrate on what your child can do, rather than what he can't – this builds confidence.
- **Do** choose situations which are relevant and interesting.
- **Do** try to put across positive attitudes about maths – your attitudes will affect your child's.
- **Do** develop you child's understanding by discussing what you are doing – *listen* to what he has to say.
- **Do** what you can to make time spent doing maths enjoyable for both of you.
- **Do** praise your child's efforts – let him see when he's made progress.
- **Don't** get disheartened by wrong answers – see them as steps in the process of learning.
- **Don't** be too quick to provide the right answers – it's understanding that is important.
- **Do** ask 'how' and 'why' questions about what your child is doing – not just 'what'. Concentrate on the thinking, not just the end result.

MATHS COMMON

When they are learning maths children have different problems at different times – these can be termed common sticking points. We've identified 12 of these – each one represents a crucial stage of learning.

This chart summarises these sticking points – you'll find fuller explanations of them on the following pages and ideas on ways you can help your child with them.

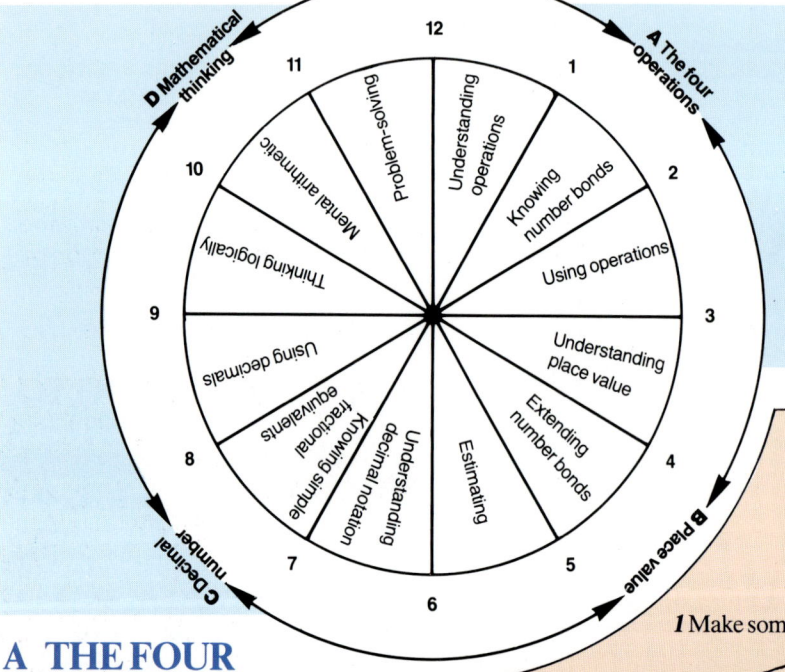

Multiplication

This is often difficult for children. *The important thing is that your child finds his own way to get the answer.*

Division

This is the most complex of the operations. Like subtraction there are two ways of thinking about it.

If you have 12 objects, you might want to 'share' them. If you want to share 12 things among three people how many will each person get?

You might, on the other hand, want to know how many groups of 3 you can make from 12. 'How many 3s in 12?'

The answer is the same – the thinking is different.

If your child has problems with any of the four operations, discuss them with his teacher and give him as much practice at home as you can in using them in real life. (See 3 below.)

2 LEARNING NUMBER BONDS

Once your child understands the operations then he can move on to the number bonds. (The term 'number bonds' is explained on page 38.) **Number bonds are facts that need to be learnt** – and then recalled with ease. You could try the game 'Beat the calculator'.

Wheel diagram with 12 segments: 1 Understanding operations, 2 Knowing number bonds, 3 Using operations, 4 Understanding place value, 5 Extending number bonds, 6 Estimating, 7 Understanding decimal notation, 8 Knowing simple fractional equivalents, 9 Using decimals, 10 Thinking logically, 11 Mental arithmetic, 12 Problem-solving. Outer labels: A The four operations, B Place value, C Decimal number, D Mathematical thinking.

A THE FOUR OPERATIONS

1 UNDERSTANDING THE OPERATIONS

Addition

Children at the 9-12 year old level generally understand the concept of addition and don't have many problems with it.

Subtraction

Children find this more difficult because there are two ways of thinking about it.

The first is 'taking away'. (If you 'take away' 3 objects from a set of 7 what is left?)

The second is 'finding the difference'. (If there are two groups, one of 7 objects, and one of 3, what is the difference between them?)

The answer is the same in both cases but the thinking is different. We use both kinds of subtraction in everyday maths.

Beat the calculator

This is a game that you can play with your child and which will help them learn their number bonds. Here's how you play it.

1 Make some cards with number bonds on them, like these.

5+8 7+3 1+9 4+7 6+7

2 Put them in a pile face down.

3 Turn over the first card. One player does the sum in his head, the other uses a calculator – who's the faster?

4 Before you turn over the next card change round.

You can add new number bonds as confidence increases. Remember, it's easy to make a mistake with a calculator, especially when you're in a hurry so some answers may need checking.

Extend the game to include subtraction, multiplication and division.

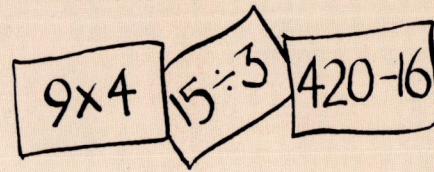

9×4 15÷3 420−16

STICKING POINTS

3 USING THE OPERATIONS

We use the four operations every day. Look for opportunities to practise them with your child. We could give examples, but taken out of context they would look off-putting and like a school maths book. You know the kind of thing – 'If I have 60p, how many 12p cakes can I buy?'

We are doing calculations of this kind all the time, especially when we are shopping. Just look for the opportunities to discuss such a calculation with your child. **It really is worth taking an extra few minutes doing the shopping** – you'll be giving your child invaluable practice.

B PLACE VALUE

4 UNDERSTANDING PLACE VALUE

Place value is a system of numbering where the position of figures is particularly important. In other words, it's 'hundreds, tens and units'. This may seem a very simple idea to you but it is a vital concept for children to

(a) Shopping provides lots of opportunities for practising maths.

understand and one which often causes problems, especially when dealing with larger numbers.

? Can your child tell you the numbers that come after 9, 99, 109, 199, 999?
? If you are looking at something for sale at £4.99 or £299, can your child tell you what the price is, to the nearest pound?
? Can your child easily add 1, 10 or 100 to a number?

You could try this activity with your child. You probably have a tape or video recorder with a digital counter. With the volume down, run the counter, fast forward, to say 199. Then press the pause button. Can your child tell you the number that comes next? If he can't tell you …

Get out some money. Find a one pound coin to represent the 1. Find nine 10p coins for the 9 in the second column, and nine 1p coins for the 9 in the last column. Ask your child to say how many pence there are. Give plenty of time for him to think about it. Now add one penny and see if he agrees that this is now 200 pence.

Go back to the digital counter and let it turn slowly to the 200.

5 EXTENDING NUMBER BONDS

If your child is to be able to learn number bonds involving larger numbers, then an understanding of place value is essential. If she has learnt $3 + 5 = 8$, can she see the similarity between that and $13 + 5 = 18$? And what about $13 + 15 = 28$? Seeing the patterns in numbers helps.

You could work out some multiplication patterns together. Here's an example:

$2 \times 3 = 6$ $20 \times 30 = 600$
$20 \times 3 = 60$ $20 \times 300 = 6000$
$200 \times 3 = 600$ $200 \times 300 = 60000$

6 ESTIMATING

We do need to have a rough idea of what the answer to a calculation is going to be. Using calculators only makes sense if we are able to anticipate an approximate answer so that we can see if we have pressed the wrong key.

(b) How long will it take to go full circle? You can talk about maths whatever you're doing!

Look for opportunities to develop your child's ability to approximate or estimate. Talk to them about 'rounding' numbers. **'I need to add 72p to 86p – that's roughly 70p and 90p, which is £1.60'.** In our everyday calculations we often don't need an answer that is more precise than this.

See if your child can help you estimate how much money you need to take to the shops to cover all the things on your list.

Being able to estimate time is useful too. You and your child could guess how long some activity is going to take – washing up, getting to the swimming pool, washing the car. If you each write down your estimate, you can check your predictions with the actual time taken.

C DECIMAL NOTATION

7 UNDERSTANDING DECIMAL NOTATION

Decimal notation is very closely linked with the concept of place value. A simple way to see this is to ask your child to add £4.23 and 51p on the calculator. If she gets the answer £55.23 then she has not keyed in 51p correctly as 0.51.

8 KNOWING SIMPLE FRACTIONAL EQUIVALENTS

This sounds complicated but all it means is that your child should be able to give the decimal version of fractions like one half, one third, quarter, etc.

Try the game of 'Calculator dominoes'.

9 USING DECIMALS

Look for opportunities to talk about the decimal numbers that we use in everyday life. There are weights and measures (what's 1.85 metres or 1.225 kg?). There's money (what is 105p?). There are the timings given on the television for sporting events (what is 9.83 seconds?).

D MATHEMATICAL THINKING

10 LOGICAL THINKING

Much of the thinking in maths may seem like common sense to you, but **children often need help in learning to think logically.** And thinking logically is what maths is all about. Play 'Twenty questions' and sharpen up your thought processes!

Twenty questions

Start by thinking of a number between 1 and 100. Your child has to find out the number by asking questions which can only be answered by 'yes' or 'no'. She will probably start by asking random questions like
- 'Is it 7?'
— 'No'
- 'Is it 19?' — 'No'

Switch round and show her how you can ask better questions like:
- 'Is it greater than 50?'
- 'Is it an odd number?'
- 'Is it less than 60?'

It should be possible to get the number after about 7 or 8 questions. It's common for a child to ask, 'Is it odd?' — 'No'; and then ask, 'Is it even?', not realising that that is an unnecessary question. Talk about this if it happens.

Calculator dominoes

1 Make a set of 12 cards like these.

0.5 / ⅓	0.333 / ¼	0.25 / ¾	0.75 / ¹⁄₁₀
0.1 / ½	0.5 / ⅔	0.666 / ⅕	0.2 / ³⁄₁₀
0.3 / ⁷⁄₁₀	0.7 / ½	0.5 / ¼	0.25 / ½

2 Share out the cards and play dominoes, matching decimals with the correct ordinary fractions.

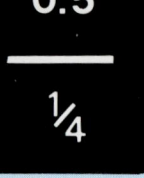

3 Check with a calculator. (To check ½ = 0.5, key in [1] [÷] [2] [=] and for ¾ = 0.75 key in [3] [÷] [4] [=])

11 MENTAL ARITHMETIC

Use every opportunity you can to practise your child's ability to do calculations in her head. You could play a version of 'Beat the Calculator' using more complex calculations this time, like
$(3 \times 4) + 2 =$
$(24 \div 2) + 3 =$
$23 + 9 + 14 =$
(Sometimes brackets help to show which calculation is to be done first.) You can't really do this as a race – one person does the calculation mentally, the other checks the answer with the calculator.

12 PROBLEM-SOLVING

All kinds of everyday problems involve mathematical thinking. Involve your child as much as you can in discussing possible solutions. What about one of these?

1 Are you planning an outing? How are you going? If it's by train or bus look at the timetable – which is the best one to choose? When do you need to leave the house? If it's by car, how long will the journey take? How much petrol should you put in the car? How much money will you need to take? Take all the suggestions your child makes seriously – if necessary explain why you can't do what she suggests, but **she just might have got a good idea!**

2 Are you planning a foreign holiday? Which one is the best value? What's the timing involved? How much foreign currency should you take? What is it worth in sterling? What should the family budget be? What does your child need money for – can he work out his own budget?

3 Are you planning a major purchase? If it's a car, involve your child in choosing the one that's the best value – look at engine capacities, fuel consumption, top speeds. If it's a domestic appliance, like a washing machine, which is the best buy? Will it fit into the kitchen? Will it be more economical than the old one?

WHAT ELSE CAN YOU DO?

Card games are good for providing practice in handling numbers.

Playing darts involves quite complex mathematical calculations.

Board games which involve scoring, using money or making any kind of mathematical judgement are useful practice too.

Getting your children involved in D.I.Y. gives them good practice in measuring.

Making a family calendar will not only help everyone know where they are supposed to be when – it will provide useful practice in recording times and dates.

Most kinds of sporting activities lend themselves to mathematical thinking. What about calculating the cricketing average for the season? What about keeping a record of how personal best times for swimming or running improve?

Does your calculator know the rules?

$3 + 2 \times 5$

It is worth finding out whether your child's calculator 'chains' calculations or just does them as they come.
Key in ③ ➕ ② ✖ ⑤ ＝

Is the answer 25?
The calculator is taking them as they come. Your child will have to know the rules to get the right answers. For this particular problem, she would need to key in

② ✖ ⑤ ＝ ➕ ③ ＝

Is the answer 13?
Lucky for some! The calculator is following the **rules of arithmetic**, working out multiplications/divisions before addition/subtraction.

Choosing THE RIGHT BOOKS

*I*n a way, there's no such thing as 'the right books' because all children will differ in needs and tastes, just as adults do. One nine-year-old might still secretly enjoy fairy stories while another might want to read nothing but books about space. What matters is to get your child reading first and then encourage her to broaden her choice. So **don't try to stop your child reading comics – you probably won't succeed anyway!** Instead, accept the comics and encourage her to read other things too. Some ways of doing this are suggested on page 26. Try not to be *too* disappointed if she isn't keen on the books you enjoyed as a child!

It might help to know what books are actually popular with 9 to 12-year-olds. In the box there's a list of the most popular fiction chosen in a recent survey.

Children should have books all around them.

NEW BOOKS

You can keep up to date with what's being published for children through your local library – ask the librarian or refer to magazines such as *Books for Keeps*, which your library should have. You can also order copies of magazines or books about children's fiction and non-fiction. Names of two good ones are given on pages 70.

WHERE CAN YOU GET BOOKS?

New books are very expensive! You don't have to spend a fortune, though, to build up a library for your child. You can get books from —

Jumble sales You can often pick up real bargains here, especially if you're an experienced jumble sale buyer and get there early!

Charity shops and secondhand book shops also often sell children's books very cheaply.

Your local library Apart obviously from lending books, many libraries now sell off their more battered books, again for a few pence. And you can work wonders with a bit of Sellotape!

Swapping with other children Make sure your child's name is clearly marked in all his books, then encourage him to lend and borrow from friends. (You may want to suggest that some books, like those bought as special presents, aren't lent.) Children are usually interested in what their friends have enjoyed reading, and may even begin talking about books too …

Book clubs e.g. Red House Book Club, Puffin Book Club, often give good advice and enable those living in outlying areas to obtain good children's books.

BUILDING A REFERENCE LIBRARY

The ideas above apply equally to fiction and non-fiction, but you have to be a bit more careful about building up a collection of reference books. If you're thinking of buying a secondhand non-fiction book, do check the date it was published. (You'll usually find this on the very first left-hand page.) Science books date very quickly, though this may not seem to matter so much with books on history or geography, for example. However, even here our ideas have changed over the years and older books may present a very different view of things.

A children's encyclopaedia, such as the Macmillan Children's Encyclopaedia, can make a good present, but you'll also need to encourage your child to use reference books in the local library or the school library. If in doubt, ask the librarians! They'll be only too pleased to help encourage young readers to become regular library users.

Title	Author	Publisher
Witch's Daughter	BAWDEN, Nina	Gollancz
What Difference Does It Make Danny?	YOUNG, Helen	Armada Books
Absolute Zero	CRESSWELL, Helen	Faber
Marmalade Atkins in Space	DAVIES, Andrew	Thames-Methuen
Bogwoppit	WILLIAMS, Ursula Moray	H Hamilton
The Cartoonist	BYARS, Betsy	Bodley Head
Grinny	FISK, Nicholas	Heinemann
Pinballs-1	BYARS, Betsy	Bodley Head
The House that Sailed Away	HUTCHINS, Pat	Armada Books
Animal Ghosts	(ed) DAVIS, Richard	Dragon Books
Witches	DAHL, Roald	Cape
Dragons Live Forever	SWINDELLS, Robert	Hodder
My Best Fiend	LAVELLE, Sheila	Armada Books
TV Kid	BYARS, Betsy	Bodley Head

YOUR CHILD'S WORLD

Dealing with anxiety	48
Relationships with other children	50
Your child's changing body	51
Building up your child's confidence	52
Encouraging independence	55
Dealing with group pressures	56
Managing the family's time	57
Making workspace for your child	58

M

WHAT IS ANXIETY?

Anxiety is a normal human response and a lot of anxiety is unavoidable. If your child has to go into hospital, the doctor's reassurance that it is a straightforward routine operation may lessen your anxiety, but nevertheless, the child will be anxious, mother will be anxious and father will be anxious.

However, parents only need to worry about anxiety in a child when it is either inappropriate or out of proportion. But this is not as simple as it seems. Here is what a normal, healthy, happy, bright eleven-year-old said were the things that were worrying him, in this order:
- getting married (Will I get married and to whom?)
- my new school (What will the new secondary school be like?)
- my job (What job will I do when I leave school?)
- my nasturtiums (How can I stop caterpillars eating them?)

The same child's mother was worried about:
- spots (on her face)
- grey hairs (on her head)
- the electricity bill (on the way)
- wet rot (on the window frames)

So anxiety in children is much the same as anxiety in adults. Children and adults are anxious about events or circumstances which they feel they can't predict or control.

As parents, we should always remember that our children do not have our knowledge or our experience. *We* know that there is not much point in worrying about marriage and career when you are only eleven; but we only know this because we have *lived through* these worries. So don't laugh at your child's worries, or she'll be less willing to talk about her more serious anxieties. Remember, her worries are just as real to her as yours are to you.

WHAT ARE THE SIGNS OF ANXIETY?

☐ not sleeping well
☐ not eating normally
☐ recurring stomach ache/headache
☐ bed-wetting
☐ inability to concentrate or persist
☐ inability to relax
☐ unusual quietness/listlessness
☐ aggressive and unruly behaviour

But checklists like this can be very misleading for two reasons.

✓ All these things can also have a medical or physical cause. All sorts of common childhood illnesses can cause poor sleep, stomach aches, odd behaviour and even bed-wetting. Children's eyesight can change as they get older, and persistent headaches may be a sign that a child needs an eye-test, rather than psycho-analysis. With any of the signs in the list, most sensible parents would first take their child to the doctor, just to make sure.

✓ The list relates to what is thought to be normal. 'Not sleeping normally' assumes that there is a normal pattern of sleep in children. But some children may need twelve hours' sleep at night, others only five!

When we speak of 'normal' behaviour what we are really talking about is the normal range of behaviour. Some children are always noisy, excitable, messy and inconsiderate. I have heard that some are not (but I'm not sure I believe it!).

What parents need to be aware of is any substantial change in their child's behaviour. If the change is worrying you, and you are not aware of a possible cause, then the first step is to have a chat with your child's teacher about your anxieties.

WHAT MAKES ANXIOUS CHILDREN?

THE FAMILY

Family problems such as death, illness, divorce, marital problems, money worries, problems at work, or unemployment can all cause anxiety in children. **Never overlook the obvious!**

> *What parents need to be aware of is any substantial change in their child's behaviour.*

If a close relative, such as a child's grandparent, is ill or dying, or if you have just lost your job, you will be anxious and your child will pick up your anxiety. Parents are often tempted, for the best of motives, to 'keep it from the children'. If you think you can hide your anxiety from the children you are simply fooling yourself.

If children do not understand what is worrying their parents, they will usually assume that, in some way, they are to blame! This will probably make children even more anxious than they would be if they understood the reason for your anxiety.

Family ambitions Probably the most common cause of anxiety in children in families where there are no serious family problems is that in some way the parents are not satisfied with the children, and children get anxious because they feel they are letting their parents down.

If the teachers at school think that the child is doing as well as she can, it may be that parents should ask themselves, 'Are we trying too hard to make our child into something different from what she is really like?'

THE SCHOOL

Your child's teacher may have unrealistic expectations of your child and sometimes it happens that a child and a teacher (or a child and another child) just do not get on with each other. If there are really serious problems at school read pages 66 and 67 to see what you can do.

There is, however, a great danger that in trying to do what you feel is best for your child you will place a greater burden of guilt on him. There are, sadly, many cases of children with minor problems, who became children with major problems because of their parents' determination to prove that their child really did have a problem. **Beware of turning your attempts to get help into a personal crusade.**

Dealing With

ANXIETY

HOW CAN YOU HELP ANXIOUS CHILDREN?

SHORT TERM ANXIETY

You can reassure the child that even if he gets nothing right it will not mean the end of civilisation as we know it, and you will still love him just as much. Never make your love conditional upon success!

If he is really overwrought, take him out for a game of football, or a walk, or a visit to the pictures, not just to take his mind off things, but to see things in perspective.

An old actors' trick to reduce stage fright, which can help to lessen short-term anxiety, is to try to push down a wall. This produces an automatic relaxation in the muscles when you stop. (**Warning** Make sure you choose a really strong wall!) It may be worth trying the technique for relaxation given below. You may think it sounds silly, but it does work!

LONG-TERM ANXIETY

Try to define the problem. This is not as simple as it sounds. 'He doesn't like school' is too vague and general to do much about. It is often worth keeping a diary of the things your child says or does which cause you concern. There may be a pattern. Make a note of what happened before the outburst or unhappiness. **It is always important to be sure of the facts**, so be sure that what you write down is what you observe, not what you think is going on.

For example, 'He hates Mrs Smith' is not a fact, it is what you think. On the other hand, 'He said to us … "I hate Mrs Smith"' is a fact (if he said it). At some stage you may be asked, 'What evidence do you have for thinking that?' It will be better if you can quote real examples.

If you need to discuss your child's anxieties with someone else, by all means make a fuss, but do it the right way. If the problem is at school, then discuss it with the school.

Above all don't try to run away from the truth. If your marriage is on the rocks, don't search desperately for a solution for your child's anxieties until you have sorted out your own life. It has to be said that most anxious children come from homes where there is anxiety, rather than from schools where there is anxiety.

If the previous paragraphs sound a bit gloomy, don't worry. Most children's anxieties *can* be sorted out. But if you do have an anxious child remember:

- always try to find something to praise
- try not to be critical or discouraging with your child
- there are no instant solutions

Helping children to overcome anxieties takes time. If your child's behaviour or self-confidence has got worse over the past six months, it may well take six months to get better!

How to relax

There is nothing mysterious or especially difficult about learning relaxation. All it takes is a little time and effort.

Try to do this yourself first – then you can teach your child.

1 Choose a time when you can be uninterrupted for 15 minutes.

2 Find a quiet room and a comfortable bed or chair.

3 Take off your shoes and remove any tight clothing, such as a belt or a tie.

4 Now try to do each of these things in turn: clench your fists, try to touch the back of your wrists to your shoulders, hunch your shoulders, press your head against the bed or chair, clench your teeth and frown hard, take a deep breath and hold it, flatten your stomach, stretch your legs and point your toes.

5 Now try to do all those things at the same time – this will mean that you are tensing all your muscles. Hold it for a slow count of 5 – feel the tension building up and up.

6 Let go completely. Keep your eyes lightly closed. Breathe quietly and evenly. Each time you breathe out feel yourself become more deeply relaxed. Imagine that a stream of clear, warm water is flowing from the top of your head, through your muscles, down your shoulders, forearms, wrists and hands and then out of the tips of your fingers; feel it pouring down your spine and chest, down your thighs, calves, ankles, feet and finally emerging from your toes. As the fluid pours through your muscles they become warmer and warmer, heavier and heavier.

THEN…

Imagine you are resting on a small cloud which is carrying you across the sky. The blue sea appears and a long golden beach. Your cloud comes down slowly on the beach. You step off onto the warm sand. You lie down on the beach.

It is a safe and peaceful place. There is nothing to fear. There is nobody to hurt you. It is quiet and gentle and belongs entirely to you.

You can return to this magic island any time you start feeling tense or anxious.

Practice relaxing three or four times a week for the first three weeks, then a couple of times each week to stay in practice. Just before going to sleep is ideal because it ensures a good night's rest.

Relationships with other children

Having friends and being able to make new friends easily are assets for any child.

While children are between the ages of 9 and 12 they undergo major changes in their lives. They will change schools, either from first to middle, or from primary to secondary. The chances are that they will be moving to a much bigger school. Having friends and being able to make new friends easily are assets which will help your child through this change.

Like adults, some children seem to make friends effortlessly; for others it is a slower and more difficult process.

You obviously can't force your child into making friends. If you are bothered by the fact that he has few or no friends then it is worth talking to him to find out whether he is as worried about it as you are. If you feel it's a delicate subject to talk about, you might find the points about 'careful listening' on page 8 helpful.

Don't make it a big issue. If your child gets the feeling that you think something must be wrong with her, then it will just make matters worse.

Your child may be able to give reasons for the lack of friends. You might be able to pick up clues for yourself by observing your child with other children.

- Sometimes children are reluctant to co-operate with others; perhaps she refuses to share her possessions?

- Maybe she tends to be aggressive if she doesn't get her way? Is she a bad loser?

If you feel either of these is true for your child, look for ways to develop her social skills, for example:

1 Try to get your child interested in some co-operative activity, like a team game.

2 Look for other activities where teamwork matters, like playing in a band, taking part in a school play. What would appeal to your child?

What else can you do?

Do encourage your child to learn a sport – it doesn't have to be a team game. Involvement of this kind will increase your child's confidence.

Do help your child make friends. A child with friends is seldom bullied.

3 Encourage your child to join a club or society. The more she mixes with other children the better.

There may be other more external reasons why your child seems to be without friends at the moment.

- Has she recently moved school or classes?
- Is there something which makes the other children regard your child as different? Children tend to reject anyone they think is different – because of an accent, appearance, interests.

Finding ways to build up your child's confidence would probably help. See pages 54 and 55.

Advise your child to hide hurt feelings. If he is being teased for being different it does help if he can laugh at a joke against himself. He's more likely to win friends doing this than if he sulks or shows that he is angry. After all, it's no fun to tease someone who doesn't seem to mind.

Suggest that your child takes something with him to do at breaktime, like a new toy or a puzzle if this is allowed by the school. This not only will cover up his loneliness but will also draw the other children like a magnet.

Is it possible for you to keep open house, so that your child knows he can invite friends to play or to tea?

IS YOUR CHILD BEING BULLIED?

Bullying is not just physical aggression. A child can be extremely distressed just by threats of aggression, by sarcasm and by persistent teasing. A bully's most likely victims are quiet children.

If you feel your child is very anxious about something and you suspect she is being bullied, do your best to talk about it with her.

If the bullying is more than a 'one-off' event, report it to the school head. **There is no reason why you and your child should have to cope with this on your own.** The head will have experience of such matters and will act in the best interests of your child. (See page 66 for what to do when things go wrong at school.)

Don't teach your child to fight back – this is playing the bully's own game.

Don't immediately complain to the bully's parents.

Your Child's Changing Body

Do any of these situations sound familiar?

- Your child has started having tantrums like a 2-year-old
- Your child is moody and doesn't seem to have any energy
- Your child gets furious if anyone enters her bedroom without permission

There *could* be *one* reason – puberty.

> ❝ *For most children puberty starts when they are over 12, but some mature physically much earlier* ❞

Is puberty making your child anxious?

◇ Puberty tends to produce an exaggerated awareness of any bodily imperfections. A spotty back, fat legs or a flat chest can be seen as monstrous deformities. Having to expose these horrors in the changing rooms at school or in the showers can be acutely distressing.

◇ Because children mature at different rates, **those who are more or less physically developed are quite likely to get teased** – and this can be a source of great anxiety.

WHAT CAN YOU DO?

First find out if your child is feeling worried about having to expose her body at school. You may find it helpful to read the section on 'careful listening' on page 8 first.

Teasing can make school changing rooms places to be dreaded.

IS PUBERTY MAKING YOUR CHILD DIFFICULT?

Puberty can cause changes in behaviour. There are great hormonal changes taking place in your child's body when he starts puberty. These can sap his energies, making him listless, apathetic and moody. He is also much more likely to answer back and to resent your authority.

Do respect your child's desire for privacy. Make it a house rule for no-one to enter anyone else's bedroom without permission.

Do try to provide factual information on sex if this seems to be what your child is anxious about. If you're not sure of the facts get a good basic textbook.

Do offer reassurance when asked for it.

Don't write to the school asking for your child to be excused from showers – he'll only get teased even more.

Don't barge into the bathroom when your child is in there – respect his need for modesty.

Don't laugh at your child's anxieties about his body. *If you can remember feeling the same, admit it and be willing to talk about it.* Reassure him that he is *not* abnormal.

WHAT CAN YOU DO?

✻ Try to avoid unnecessary confrontations, especially over minor matters. It helps if you can be flexible and it won't reduce your authority.

✻ It's a good idea to keep family rules to a minimum – but enforce those you do have firmly and consistently. Talk about *why* you have these rules.

✻ Shouting matches generally do no good. If your child loses her temper it's not easy to keep yours. If you feel your temper rising it will help if you can just leave the room until it's back under control. Stay as calm as you can until your child's anger has passed.

✻ If your child has lost her temper, it can help to talk about it afterwards. She will probably feel guilty and miserable and talking about what happened will help her to cope with the feelings which are both powerful and frightening.

✻ Accept any apology offered – don't be tempted to have the last word. Be prepared to accept that you may have acted or spoken hastily, and apologise *yourself*.

✻ *Your child is trying to grow up. It's not an easy business* – be as placid and as reassuring as you can be.

51

BUILDING UP YOUR

There's probably no such thing as the totally confident child – the child who is articulate, self-assured, sociable and emotionally resilient; who asks many questions and is always ready to suggest answers; who tackles difficult tasks with enthusiasm; and who learns from mistakes. Come to think of it, how many adults do you know like that?

Most children will be more confident in some situations than others. Some children do go through stages when they seem to be generally lacking in self-confidence. If you feel your child is one of these, you could start by ticking those statements which seem to be true of your child.

☐ Acts on her own initiative.
☐ Takes the lead when playing with friends.
☐ Joins in group activities willingly.
☐ Stands up for herself in an argument.
☐ Is not too upset by criticism.
☐ Has a cheerful outlook.
☐ Enjoys visiting new places on holiday.
☐ Makes her own decisions.
☐ Accepts challenges with enthusiasm.
☐ Is generally optimistic.

Score:
7-10 ticks – your child has above average self-confidence
4-6 ticks – your child has average self-confidence
1-3 ticks – your child tends to lack confidence

Remember: hardly anyone is always cheerful and no-one *likes* being criticised, so don't be too concerned if you've only been able to tick one or two of these statements.

Feeling confident is all tied up with our feelings about ourselves – our self-image.

WHAT MAKES A GOOD SELF-IMAGE?

There are two things which contribute towards a good self-image – *our sense of competence* and *our sense of self-esteem*.

If you want to explore your child's self-image here are some things you can do.

1 Find out how he regards his own school performance. Here is a game called 'Where are you?' Get your child to draw himself inside – or colour in – the appropriate box.

This is the WHERE ARE YOU? game. Draw a stick man to show where you believe you are when you compare yourself to how others behave in life.
I believe I am . . .

	5 marks	3 marks	1 mark	0	
Very hard working	☻				Not very hardworking
Very good at learning		☻			Not very good at learning
Very good at maths				☻	Not very good at maths
Very good at writing	☻				Not very good at writing
Very good at reading	☻				Not very good at reading
Very good at tests				☻	Not very good at tests
A very good student		☻→☻			Not a very good student
Liked by my teachers		☻	☻		Not liked by my teachers
Successful in school			*		Not successful in school
Clever			☻	☻	Not very clever

* What have I done that is a credit to the school? I haven't been in a school play for two whole

CHILD'S CONFIDENCE

For every stick man marked in the left-hand column give 5 points, for each one in the next column 3 points, the next 1 and the last 0.
Score:
26-50 high
17-25 medium
10-16 low

Make sure you 'score' the game when your child is not around. Don't worry too much if his score seems to be low – there are things you can do to help. Remember this is how *your child* views his performance. How do you think it relates to the realities – is he badly under-rating himself? Or indeed is he over-rating his performance? Both would be quite normal things for children to do.

2 How does she regard herself? Have you often heard your child say any of these things? Tick those that seem to be true of your child.

☐ I often feel lonely at school.
☐ My friends are always going off to play with someone else.
☐ I feel silly when I'm talking to teachers.
☐ I don't like answering questions – it makes me feel stupid.
☐ Other people don't like me.
☐ I dislike team games.
☐ There are lots of things about me that I would change if I could.

If you ticked *any* of these then your child's self-image is not all it should be.

You won't necessarily find that a low competence rating and a low self-image go together. Some children can have a good image of themselves but not be very good at academic subjects. This is often the case when they are good at other things like sport or music or drama. If your child comes into this category then you could look at ways to increase classroom competence.

Self-image in the classroom

You can find two kinds of child in any classroom – the 'can't knowers' and the 'don't knowers'.

The 'don't knowers' will admit that they don't understand something and will then proceed to solve the problem.

The 'can't knowers' admit that they cannot understand, but really think they will *never* understand.

For the 'don't knowers' the world is filled with possibilities. For 'can't knowers' it's full of impossibilities.

The most important difference between the two kinds of children is self-image.

Some children can be very competent in school but have a very poor image of themselves. This is often the case where a child feels inadequate outside school. One clever girl, for example, counted her classroom success as nothing compared to her inability to be popular with boys. If your child comes into this category then you could look at ways to build up your child's self-image and confidence.

Taking part in sports can do a lot to help build confidence.

IMPROVING YOUR CHILD'S COMPETENCE

You could use the *Success!* Activity and Practice books to improve basic skills in reading, writing and maths.

It might be helpful to look at 'Helping your child want to learn' on pages 17 and 18.

53

IMPROVING YOUR CHILD'S SELF-ESTEEM

Here are some ways you can help.

> *If I get the answer right in a test I know it must have been very easy.*

This is the attitude of a child who is actually very competent but refuses to believe it. Could it be true for your child?

1 Try this technique – your child won't believe you if you tell her she has done well, but she's more likely to believe it if she hears you telling someone else. You could ensure that your child 'accidentally' hears you talking to your partner or another respected adult. We all tend to believe that people are more honest about us when they talk behind our backs!

2 The GIGO bank GIGO is a word borrowed from the world of computers. It stands for 'garbage in, garbage out'. It is used to remind computer programmers that a computer is only as good as the programs it is given. *If you feed garbage into the machine, then garbage is all it will produce.*

Here 'garbage' refers to the negative comments which some adults make frequently about their children. Ten of the most frequent are:

✗ Do as I say – not as I do!
✗ Why can't you do as well as …?
✗ You'll never amount to anything!
✗ Don't be stupid!
✗ Can't you do anything right?
✗ You are so lazy!
✗ You're too young to do that!
✗ Always ask me first.
✗ Why? Because I say so!
✗ You are such a disappointment!

These comments and negative words like 'dumb', 'stupid', etc. are **GIGO**.

Of course all of us use these from time to time. The danger arises when such comments become a habit. The child is being regularly told that he is inferior. After a time these comments become 'internalised' and the child believes the comments to be true. The damage to his self-esteem can be considerable.

If you feel you have fallen into this habit, then here's a way to break it.

Make a **GIGO bank**. This is a container with a slot at the top. With the help of your child, write out any GIGO comments which you often make.

Fasten the list of GIGO comments to the front of the box. If you make any of the comments, your child should say 'GIGO'. If you agree that it's that kind of comment, put an agreed sum of money in the GIGO bank. When the total sum reaches a reasonable amount, you could spend it together on some activity you both enjoy.

> There is a difference between GIGO comments and valid criticism e.g. *'You are bone idle,'* is a GIGO comment. *'From what the teacher says about your homework, you don't seem to have made enough effort. What went wrong?'* is quite a valid thing to say.

If you're not sure whether a comment is GIGO or not, ask yourself, 'Would I like it if someone said that to me and meant it to be taken seriously?'

You might think that this sounds far too elaborate to do – but has it set you thinking?

3 Getting the balance right – rewards and punishments Frequent **punishment** can undermine a child's feelings of self-esteem. *Punish only when you are certain that it is justified.* Try not to punish as a way of venting your feelings of irritation or frustration over something that has nothing to do with your child.

For example, you might have had an awful day at work. You come home and raise hell with your children for leaving their bedrooms in a mess. Their bedrooms might indeed be in an awful state but what you are really doing is venting your anger on your children *instead of* your boss or colleagues.

If you realise that you have been unreasonable, it isn't too late. Come clean! Explain that you've had a bad day, admit you're in a bad mood. Let your child see how to cope with their *own* unreasonable behaviour.

Reward by praising, showing your approval, taking an interest, offering your support. Such actions may do more for your child's esteem than costly material rewards.

Becoming your own person is important.

REWARD FAR MORE OFTEN THAN YOU PUNISH

Encouraging INDEPENDENCE

A child who has a poor self-image may benefit from being given rather more independence.

You might find it useful to take yourself through this short list of statements. Score your reactions like this:

You strongly agree with the statement – 5 points
You agree – 4 points
You neither agree or disagree – 3 points
You disagree – 2 points
You strongly disagree – 1 point

Parents should

- [ ] make their child's life as trouble-free as possible
- [ ] shield their child from disappointments
- [ ] always know what their child is thinking
- [ ] always know exactly what their child is doing
- [ ] take important decisions on behalf of their child
- [ ] expect complete loyalty from their child
- [ ] never let their child question parental judgements
- [ ] never tolerate criticism from their child
- [ ] expect total obedience from their child
- [ ] feel free to read their child's private diary
- [ ] be able to enter their child's bedroom without permission
- [ ] not discuss their child's feelings with them
- [ ] not let their child see distressing TV programmes
- [ ] not let children get their way too often
- [ ] demand respect from their children
- [ ] make every sacrifice for their child
- [ ] inspire a healthy fear in their child
- [ ] never show their emotions in front of their children
- [ ] make sure their child works hard
- [ ] always have the last say in any important decision

Score:
20-35 *You allow your child a great deal of freedom*
36-50 *You allow your child a moderate amount of independence*
51-75 *You are reluctant to allow your child much freedom*
76-100 *You allow your child almost no freedom*

All parents want to protect their children from harm and distress. Restricting a child's freedom does not imply any lack of warmth or love. In fact a parent's desire to shield her child from life's dangers and disappointments probably indicates very understandable concern. It is *important*, however, that children should be allowed to face up to the problems of living, that they should make mistakes, get into and out of difficulties, experience disappointment, feel the pain of rejections and cope with 'normal, human unhappiness'.

By allowing your child to experience more of the world, *within a caring and loving family*, you are more likely to encourage the development of an assertive, self-reliant and independent-minded person.

If your child is over-protected, he may well grow up quiet and well-behaved, but he may also be too passive. There are real dangers in this. **Excessively dependent children are at the mercy of others,** whether they be parents, teachers or other children – their self-esteem can be shattered so easily. They may also be easily influenced by other children. (See page 56.)

If you feel you don't give your child enough freedom, what can you do?

▶ Look at the rules you impose on the family. Are there a lot? Try to retain *only* those which are necessary to safeguard your children and your home from physical danger, and you from insanity!

▶ **Apply those rules you do keep as consistently as possible.** If you are tempted to bend rules 'just this once' your child may become confused or will realise that, with enough pleading or grumbling, you can be persuaded to change your mind. This will lead to more pleading and grumbling next time!

▶ Trust your child and make it clear that you do so.

▶ Try seeing the world through your child's eyes.

▶ Involve your child actively in family decision-making. Instead of saying what is going to be done and when, ask for suggestions, ideas and advice. Take those suggestions seriously – your child will soon realise if you are patronising her. Your child must feel that she's able to influence the outcome. If the idea your child has is *really* unworkable, explain why and see whether she can come up with a more realistic alternative.

If you feel you allow too much freedom, what can you do?

If your child has freedom within a caring and loving family, he is unlikely to come to harm. Talk about the need for rules with your child – he'll probably see the sense in having some. Most children prefer to know how they should behave.

55

DEALING WITH GROUP
PRESSURES

Would your child be able to say no?

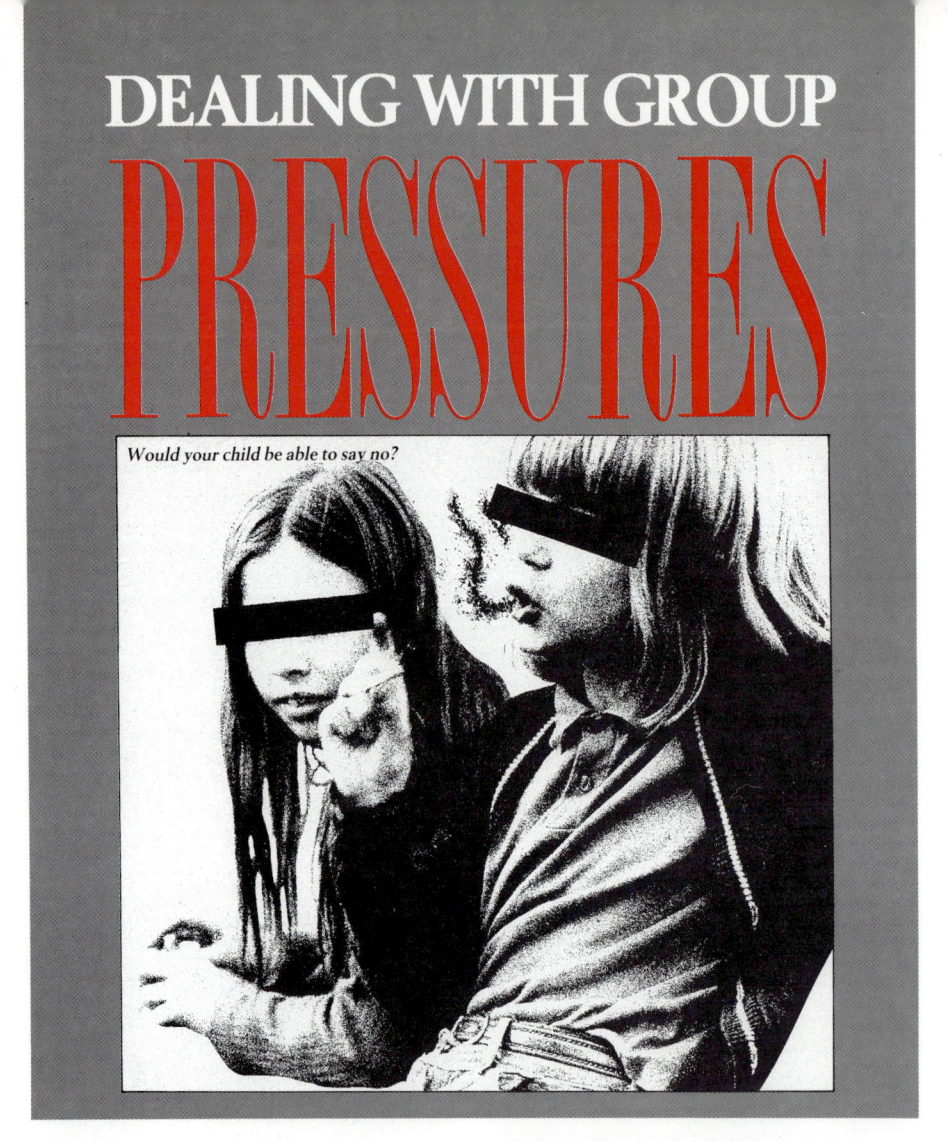

Almost always a child gets into trouble *with other children, not on their own.*

WHAT KIND OF TROUBLE?

USING BAD LANGUAGE, SMOKING

Your child will almost certainly hear bad language being used by other children at school. He may even use it without really knowing what it means. **The chances are high that he will be offered a cigarette.** The pressures on him to be 'bad' may be hard to withstand. No-one wants to be rejected, no-one wants to be thought a coward, no-one wants to be called a 'sissy'. **Would your child be able to say no?**

BEING A BULLY, PLAYING TRUANT

These are less likely to happen to your child. If, however, he has become part of a group which is dominated by a child who is aggressive, anti-school, probably physically mature, then drifting into this kind of behaviour is possible, even for the previously well-behaved child. **Would your child refuse to be part of such a group?**

STEALING AND OTHER ILLEGAL ACTIVITIES

Again, if she is affected by a group of children who regard it as exciting to break the rules, even a well-brought up child can find herself taking absurd risks and attempting things which, in saner moments, she would realise were foolish and wrong. **Would your child be able to walk away when she knows things have gone too far?**

GROUP ATTITUDES

Children, like adults, are far more likely to behave badly when they are part of a group than when they are on their own. Each can then blame the others; it's not necessary to take individual responsibility. **And the charms of being accepted as part of a group are considerable.**

As part of a group your child might go along with attitudes, might express opinions, which he would never dream of adopting at home. He might, for example, join in taunting children of other races; he might join in frightening an elderly person; he might join in the laughter directed at a person in a wheelchair. **Would your child continue to respect the rights of others even at the cost of being rejected by his peers?**

WHAT CAN YOU DO TO HELP?

You may be tempted into believing that it is the child who is allowed too much freedom that is likely to be led astray by others. You may feel, that if you have an obedient and dutiful child, she will not get into trouble.

In fact the opposite is often the case. **The very obedient child may find it more difficult to say no to others.** The very loyal child may transfer her loyalty to the charismatic leader of the group. The child who has had no experience in making her own decisions, in developing her own sense of responsibility, is less likely to be able to withstand the pressures of the group.

REMEMBER

- **Do** encourage your child to be independent in thought and action. Read the section on encouraging independence on page 55.
- **Do** help your child accept responsibility for his decisions by, for example, letting him choose the food he eats, letting him wear the kind of clothes he wants around the house, decorating his room the way he wants.
- **Do** try to create the strong self-discipline that is your child's best defence against unwelcome influence. One way of doing this is to keep the number of rules in your home to a minimum. But don't do without them altogether. Children do need a clear framework of rules by which to evaluate their conduct.
- **Do** apply the rules you do have *consistently.* If you sometimes allow conduct which is punished on other occasions, your child may become increasingly contemptuous of adult authority.
- **Do** explain your rules. Don't just impose them. Never try to justify an order with the statement, 'Because I say so …'. This fosters the unquestioning attitude which an unscrupulous group leader may later exploit.
- **Do** try to encourage your child to ask, 'Why?' instead of meekly accepting an adult's decisions. This may not always make her popular at school or at home, but it is still a far healthier response than blind acceptance of authority.
- **Do** what you can to foster the right kind of friendships for your child. Encourage your child to bring friends home to tea or to play.

MANAGING The Family's TIME

At this stage you may well be wondering how you can possibly fit all this in! You may feel that it's quite difficult enough to find the time to sit down and help your child with his maths, reading or writing. And you may say, 'It's all very well telling me to listen carefully to what my child is saying, and be patient and understanding – **have you any idea of what goes on in our house?'**

Lots of families with children in this age group and over have amazingly complicated timetables pinned up on kitchen walls. Daily life is dominated by logistics. Does this sound familiar?

> David needs to be at basketball practice by 6 and Sarah needs to be collected from her music lesson at 6.15. Dad's working late. Sixteen-year-old Susi wants her meal early so that she can go round to her boyfriend's and Mum has to do her German homework before her evening class at 7.30.

With family commitments like these fitting in the time to spend half an hour with David each day helping him with maths may look out of the question.

Time together is important.

WHAT ABOUT TIME FOR RELAXING?

It may not be just a matter of finding the time for a home learning scheme. With all the family involved in all kinds of activities, when do both grown ups and children have the chance to rest? Do your children eventually flop down in front of the television? And do you and your partner eventually do the same – and immediately go off to sleep? We would all probably enjoy having some relaxed time with the kids but somehow it only seems possible at the weekends or during holidays.

CAN YOU FIND ANY EXTRA TIME?

WHAT CAN BE DROPPED?

When you're next drawing up a family timetable or filling in the diary or making lists or whatever it is that your family does to show who's doing what when, try talking it through with the whole family first. It might be an idea to get the children to write out the timetable – see if they can spot the time clashes and the times when Dad gets five minutes to eat his tea and Mum has to get the tea ready in less! Is there any regular time when everybody can relax together and talk about the day they've had?

If you're thinking of using a home learning scheme with one of your children, talk about how you and your child will find the time for it. As we've mentioned before, it's only a matter of finding 20 minutes or so but it should really be a quiet and relaxed time – not time that's been grabbed.

Perhaps one of your child's activities could be dropped – at least for a time? Maybe your child would like to suggest an activity you could drop as well!

WHAT ABOUT LESS TELEVISION?

It might be possible to reduce the amount of time your child (and you?) spend watching television. *It's so easy to use television as a form of relaxation* but the chances are that neither your child nor you would mind missing a programme or two if the alternative was to spend some relaxed and interesting time together.

Why not get your child to draw up her ideal viewing timetable for the week and get her to work out how many hours it is. She'll be practising some useful reading and maths skills while she does it! When she's done it, discuss with her the programmes which she could miss without undue misery and which would give her an extra half hour a day. Agree with her that the television gets turned off when the chosen programmes are over. Of course that's easier said than done if you have several children each with a list of favourite programmes. In that case, you and your child will have to seek refuge in a quiet room in the house.

CAN YOU DELEGATE ANY CHORES?

If the person who's really having problems fitting in home learning sessions is you, can you get the family to help out with some of your chores? Persuading one other member of the family to take over the washing up, for example, could give you just the time you need to sit down and look at what one of your children has done in their home learning scheme.

WILL THE TIME BE RESPECTED?

It's all too easy, even when you and your child have agreed on a particular time, for distractions to occur. The phone goes, your toddler falls over, your neighbour looks in. If all the family knows that the time you are spending together with your child is important and should, wherever possible, be safeguarded, then maybe someone else will deal with the distractions. And *it could do wonders for an unconfident child to know that your time with him takes priority*, whenever possible, over other things.

MAKING WORKSPACE FOR YOUR CHILD

DESIGNING AND PLANNING

Ideally, when designing a child's bedroom, try to keep the studying area separate from the sleeping area. Keep the design uncluttered and simple, leaving as much open space as possible.

When children have to share bedrooms, this can cause problems. Try to give each child clearly defined areas, by organising the furniture to give each one his own space. If the room is large enough, you could separate the areas with curtains, screens or double-sided bookshelves. Give each child his own bedside lamp.

If the room just doesn't lend itself to separate areas, at least set out the furniture so that they don't each feel overlooked by the other. Perhaps the beds could go at right angles to each other, a wardrobe could be placed strategically to give some privacy.

DECORATING THE ROOM

Allowing a child to have a say in choosing the decorating scheme for her room is always a good idea, but be prepared to intervene to avoid disasters. The 'fairy' wallpaper which delights a 5-year-old may be an embarrassment at 8.

It is *her* study area, though, so *do* involve her in choosing colour schemes and furnishings.

Plan for the future. Remember, the room has to 'grow' with your child – and as economically as possible. So avoid special child desks and mini-beds.

Don't forget the computer!

If space is limited think about this bed and desk combination.

Shelving and storage space are essential.

Essentials

Check this list for your child's study bedroom.

Warmth	Most central heating systems are designed to provide lower temperatures in bedrooms than in other parts of the house. Check, and adjust if necessary.
Lighting	Make the most of both natural and artificial lighting. Place the desk under the window? A single centre light is probably not adequate.
Storage	He needs space to keep his mess tidy! Think about large, plastic stacking boxes, or underbed drawers.
Shelving	He needs lots of it! Fit inexpensive adjustable shelving, or even Dexion shelves.
Power points	There are never enough. As well as lights, he'll need outlets for computers, radios, etc. Consider using a purpose-built multi-socket extension lead.
Pinboards	Give him room to display favourite posters and good work!
Safety note	Check wiring and points properly. Fix shelves – free-standing ones especially – securely so they can't fall over.

YOU AND YOUR CHILD'S SCHOOL

Meeting the teacher	60
The world of school	62
Choosing the right school	65
What do you do when things go wrong?	66
How to get more involved	68
Where to get further advice	70
Detailed assessment for your child	72
Where to find out about	72

M

Meeting the Teacher

Many parents can feel very apprehensive about having contact and discussions with their child's teacher(s), for a variety of reasons. But what about teachers? How might *they* feel about meeting the parents of their pupils with, for example, the prospect of parents' evening coming up?

The Parent | The Teacher

Parent A has absolute faith in the teachers at his son's school because they are trained professionals who 'know all there is to know'. He is very intimidated at meeting them because they are experts and he is not.

The teacher is very concerned about Mr A. On a previous parents' evening, he hardly spoke at all and whatever he said to him got very little response. He can't make up his mind whether Mr A is unhappy with his son's progress, quite content or simply doesn't care very much.

WHAT COULD PARENT A DO?
Tell the teacher how he feels, say, for example; 'I'm pleased about the way you say Adam is getting on and I'd like to thank you for what you've done to help him.'

Parent B was not terribly successful at school himself and remembers teachers as seemingly all-powerful beings who did nothing to alleviate his own rather unhappy schooldays. These memories and impressions of his own time at school make him very reluctant to talk to his child's teachers whom he assumes are like the ones he used to know.

The teacher knows nothing about the father's background other than that he runs a small building firm. He hasn't been to parents' evenings previously, so the teacher believes he is unlikely to come this time. She assumes he is either too busy (really?) or that he is not interested in his child's progress and education.

WHAT COULD PARENT B DO?
Give the teacher the benefit of the doubt! Go along and say, for example, 'I'm sure things have changed a lot since I was at school . . . please could you explain how you teach maths these days?' or 'I'm really pleased that Becky seems so happy at school, how is her work coming along?

Parent C is a teacher herself although at a different school. She therefore knows a great deal about education – more, probably, than her child's teacher who has only been teaching for two years. Parent C is worried that she will appear to be an interfering 'teacher parent' or undermine the class teacher because of her own knowledge/professional background.

The teacher knows that Chris's mum is also a teacher and, although slightly nervous, she is looking forward to talking to her about Chris's work because they can use the same terminology and they both fully understand the day to day work and pressures of the classroom. From this base of shared experience they can have a fruitful discussion about Chris's work and progress since they will both be looking forward to the meeting.

WHAT COULD PARENT C DO?
Come clean with the teacher and explain her anxieties. Perhaps she could say, 'I'm very pleased with the way Chris is progressing but if there is anything you feel we should be doing to help at home, I'd really welcome your advice.'

Isn't it amazing how easily misconceptions can arise? Parents may perceive teachers in a certain way and believe that teachers will have certain perceptions about them. Teachers can perceive parents in a certain way and believe that parents will hold certain views about them. All too often the result may be a mismatch of perceptions!

SO WHAT CAN YOU DO?

Take every opportunity to *talk* to your child's teachers – misperceptions can only be adjusted by communicating!

Don't be nervous of your child's teacher. Remember:

● She might be just as nervous of meeting you.

● Even if he is an expert, you are an expert too – you've known your child a lot longer than anyone else has!

Teachers are interested in you because you are the parent of the child they are teaching. They *want* you to be interested too because with your support they can help your child more effectively.

In the unlikely event that your child's teacher should turn out to be every bit as fearsome, awe-inspiring and intimidating as in your very *worst* imaginings, remember one thing... he or she is a human being too and human beings all have features in common – that immaculate coiffure, for example, has to be washed and dried just like yours!

If you are still unhappy, read page 66 on 'What do you do when things go wrong?'

HOW DO YOU START?

Here are a few example comments and questions to get things going.

IF YOU ARE PLEASED WITH YOUR CHILD'S PROGRESS...

❛I'm really pleased at how well Angela is doing and I'm very grateful for all your hard work.❜

❛Tony seems to be doing really well with you – how do you feel things are going?❜

❛We're very happy with the way Julie is progressing – is there anything we should be doing to help even more?❜

IF YOU ARE NOT HAPPY...

❛I know you'll have noticed, too, that Ian seems to have a problem with his spelling. Could you tell me how bad it is, and if there is anything I could do to help whatever it is that you are doing in school?❜

❛We're both very worried about the way Shona seems to have lost interest in maths and we wondered if you had noticed it too? Is she having any particular difficulties?❜

Golden rules for nervous parents...

☛ Wear something that you feel comfortable in, and which you feel does you justice, to occasions like parents' evenings.

☛ Think about what you want to know and what you want to say beforehand – jot it down if it helps.

☛ Remember that it is only another human being that you are going to meet and *not* an alien or a fearsome beast!

☛ When it's your turn, take a deep breath, smile, say, 'Hello,' and say who you are. That will probably start the teacher talking.

☛ Remember that the teacher is probably worn out, dying for a cup of tea and, like any other person, appreciates praise or gratitude.

❛I'd be very grateful if you wouldn't mention to Billy that we've spoken to you about this, but he does seem to be getting increasingly unhappy about going to school each day. Have you any idea what might be wrong? We've tried asking him in a roundabout way but he won't say that anything is wrong.❜

IF YOU DON'T KNOW HOW THINGS ARE GOING...

❛Edward never seems to tell us much about school so we've very little idea about how he is getting on.❜

❛I've really been looking forward to talking to you. Mandy doesn't say much at all about school and I don't know if that's a good or a bad sign! How do you feel she is doing?❜

❛Marik is an only child so we've no idea if the standard of his work is about right for his age or not; please could you give us some guidance?❜

Teachers are interested in you because you are the parent of the child they are teaching.

the WORLD of SCHOOL

The world of school is a very real one but it is unlike any other. It figures prominently in all our lives at some stage and education is often the subject of heated debate on television, across the dinner table or in the bar – as well as in school staffrooms!

Parents rightly feel concerned about education, wanting, as they do, the best for their children. Teachers, too, are just as concerned. Most adults, be they parents, teachers, politicians or employers, recognise the importance of the school years as a springboard into adult life – better education means a wider range of options and opportunities.

THE TEACHER'S WORLD

Many adults would regard themselves as minor experts on education simply because they have experienced it at first hand. That experience, however, is not always relevant. **Everything in life changes and schools are no exception.** They are very different today, from what they were even 10 or 15 years ago. Now, for example, the teaching is more informal and discussion plays an important part as children work and learn together in small groups; the emphasis is on the pupil as an active pursuer of her own learning, rather than someone sitting passively accepting and absorbing (or not!) given facts. Teachers nowadays are much more aware of the need to teach children *how* to learn – which will equip them to deal with the rest of their lives.

Individual teachers have a very wide range of duties and responsibilities and their workload is most certainly not restricted to term times and the hours in which your child is at school! The week described on this page is by no means an exaggerated example.

Over and above all the normal range of duties and responsibilities, teachers are currently facing a time of great change as a result of the new Education Reform Act passed in 1988.

Work for the week!
1. Teaching.
2. Lesson preparation
3. Marking.
4. Put up new classroom display.
5. Arrange next term's geography field trip for 4B.
6. Order new books (How much money left to spend? Check!)
7. Make appointment to discuss John's progress with Mr. and Mrs. B. (Check with Sue, Educational Welfare Officer that Mr. B is still at home).
8. Staff meeting Tues. 4 p.m.
9. Write report on W.S. for educational psychologist.
10. Department meeting Thursday 4.30 p.m.
11. Begin end of term reports? N.B. parent's evening 21st.
12. Write letter for 2A parents re trip to Roman Baths.
13. Check tutor group's contributions for sponsored walk.
14. Talk to Head about going on the course at the University next year (Remember to ask Mike if he can arrange to be home every Wed. evening for the kids?!)

THE EDUCATION REFORM ACT — A NEW ERA?

This new parliamentary act has introduced major changes on how schools are organised and managed.

Since their first introduction in the proposed bill, all the points below have been the subject of much debate and strong views have been expressed on both sides of any fence – be it political, educational, religious or whatever.

All changes are significant but the two which will probably have most impact for teachers and pupils are the **national curriculum** and related assessment.

Major changes and introductions

- A national curriculum for all school aged children in maintained schools
- Testing of pupils at around the ages of 7, 11, 14 and 16
- An end to artificial limits on parents' first choice of schools (i.e. places at schools can be refused only if the school is actually full and not because the local education authority has set a ceiling on the number of available places each year)
- Control of school budgets to be handed over to the governors of larger primary schools and all secondary schools
- Changes to the funding and management of polytechnics and universities
- Schools with more than 300 pupils may apply to become grant-maintained and opt out of LEA control
- A compulsory daily act of collective worship in schools which should in the main be Christian and special status given to religious education
- The plans for city technology colleges to include CTCs which will specialise in the arts as well as the originally planned specialisation in maths, science and technology. These industry-sponsored establishments are intended to extend the choice of secondary education in urban areas

THE NATIONAL CURRICULUM

> ❝...all pupils will receive an education which is broad, balanced, relevant to their needs and set in a clear, moral framework.❞
>
> *Taken from the Dept. of Education and Science booklet* Education Reform, 1987

Prior to the introduction of a national curriculum, the curriculum in schools has been determined at school level within broad guidelines laid down by the local education authority (LEA). Over the years there has been a series of government-instigated reports or initiatives which have influenced this (e.g. guidance on the teaching of maths or reading, furthering computer education). What is taught and the teaching approaches used in schools is monitored by local advisors or inspectors and HMI (Her Majesty's Inspectorate – an independent, national body of experts).

The idea of a national curriculum came about because of the Government's belief that there are too many pupils underachieving in schools and that for some pupils in some schools, the curriculum is too narrow. A national curriculum is intended to guarantee that all pupils receive an education as described in the quotation above.

WHAT IS THE NATIONAL CURRICULUM?

The national curriculum will:
Establish the overall content of much of what children will learn up to the age of 16 in state maintained schools in England and Wales.
Require that pupils study three *core subjects* (English, maths and science) and seven other *foundation subjects* (history, geography, technology, art, music, physical education and, for secondary school pupils, a modern foreign language. For pupils in Wales, Welsh will become a foundation subject in non-Welsh speaking schools).
Provide attainment targets and assessment at around the ages of 7, 11, 14 and 16 (see page 64).

The national curriculum will not:
Stipulate how a school should organise its timetable, its teaching methods or the textbooks it should use.
Stipulate how much time should be spent in studying the core and foundation subjects – given, of course, that the amount of time devoted to each is sufficient to enable pupils to meet the prescribed attainment targets.

Children are now active participants in their own learning.

SOME IMPLICATIONS

The core and foundation subjects do not have to make up the complete school timetable; there should be room for other things as well. There *must*, indeed, be room for religious education. The 1944 Education Act required schools to provide religious education for all pupils in maintained schools unless they were withdrawn by their parents from such lessons. This Act is still in force and the new one, it is argued, strengthens the old in that it gives parents clearer rights to complain if they feel their child is not receiving the religious education required by law.

Many teachers, however, are concerned that there will be insufficient time left over from the teaching requirements of the core and foundation subjects to allow those such as home economics and classics to be adequately covered. It is too early, however, to say whether or not these fears will be justified.

Change, especially major change, is usually worrying for all concerned and the kind of educational change we now face is unsettling for teachers, parents and anyone connected with education in any way.

When do the changes come into effect?

Opting out of LEA control:	Immediately
City technology colleges:	The first in September 1988
RE as part of the basic curriculum:	September 1988
End to artificial limits on school places:	September 1990
Change of control over school budgets:	by April 1993 (Inner London, April 1994)
The national curriculum and attainment targets:	
September 1989:	maths, English and science for 5 year olds
	maths and science for 12 year olds
September 1990:	maths, science and English for 8 year olds

REMEMBER

- there is an obvious desire to make things work and to improve standards
- teachers have often been faced with educational changes and have always overcome the challenges involved
- teachers have been promised that they will receive in-service training to help them implement the new measures
- the changes do not all take immediate effect; there is a period of preparation.

Introduction of national tests

Tests in maths, science and English for 7 year olds	1991 (not reported)
Tests in maths, science and English for 7 year olds	1992 (reported, so you will know the results)
Tests in maths, science and English for 14 year olds	1992 (not reported)
Tests in maths, science and English for 14 year olds	1993 (reported)
Tests in maths, science and English for 11 year olds	1995 (reported)

Tests in other subjects will be phased in over the next 10 years. Technology will be one of the earliest to follow those above.

The Act states that the national curriculum and related aspects will specify:

(a) the knowledge, skills and understanding which pupils of different abilities and maturities are expected to have by the end of each key stage (attainment targets)

(b) the matters, skills and processes which are required to be taught to pupils of different abilities and maturities during each key stage (programmes of study)

(c) the arrangements for assessing pupils at or near the end of each key stage for the purpose of ascertaining what they have achieved in relation to the attainment targets for that stage.'

ASSESSMENT AND ATTAINMENT TARGETS

The idea is that attainment targets will be set for the core and foundation subjects which will give guidance as to what pupils can be expected to know and understand at about the ages of 7, 11, 14 and 16.

The Act also states that it is the Secretary of State's duty to 'establish a complete national curriculum as soon as is reasonably practicable (taking first the core subjects and then the other foundation subjects.)'

The responsibility of deciding the content of the national curriculum, attainment targets, programmes of study and assessments has been given to subject or assessment working parties appointed by the Government. These groups then prepare reports which are discussed and, after the period of consultation, accepted or otherwise by the Secretary of State.

The Task Group on Assessment and Testing published their reports in 1988. The Government has decided that its first priority is to be given to the development of assessment tasks for 7-year-olds.

The Task Group recommended that
★ There should be ten levels of performance or attainment identified for each subject which would span all ages.
★ Pupils would progress through these levels at different rates depending on their individual performance.
★ Assessment at any of the four given ages would report on which level the pupil had reached at that time.
★ Children assessed as achieving a given level would have satisfied the criteria for that level and be working towards meeting the criteria of the next.
★ One level would be roughly equivalent to about two years of educational progress. The average expectation for an 11-year-old, therefore, would be Level 4 and for a 14-year-old, Level 5/6. This is not to say that all 11-year-olds would achieve Level 4 – some would achieve less and some more, in the same way that amongst any given class of pupils there is a wide range of achievement which varies from subject to subject. For example:
★ Levels 1-3 would be used for the national assessment at age 7
★ Level 1 in a subject would identify those children who are experiencing some difficulty while those at Level 3 would have made much speedier progress
★ On the same scale, for the same subject, older pupils who at 16 reach Levels 9/10 could be said to be achieving the equivalent of the top grades in GCSE examinations.

It is important to remember that whilst children will be assessed at the national reporting ages of 7, 11, 14 and 16, teachers will continue as they have always done to make their own assessments of children's progress during the intervening periods.

THE NATURE OF THE ASSESSMENTS

It has been proposed that the assessments for children at ages 7 and 11 should be similar in form to their normal school work. There would, therefore, be much cross-curricular overlap between subject areas – just as there is in normal primary work where the study of one topic brings in skills and information from several curricular areas. (For example, learning about chocolate brings in English, maths, history, geography, and so on.)

The assessment tasks will come from a national bank of such tasks but will be administered and marked by teachers. Not all would necessarily be 'pencil and paper' tasks -- some may be practical activities requiring observation from the teacher. Results of the tasks and the teacher's assessments would make up an individual attainment profile for each child.

Of necessity, this introduction to the new assessment plans has to be brief and general. Without all the subject working groups' reports, their acceptance by Government and time to devise and trial assessment tasks, we cannot, at present, state with any kind of certainty exactly what the new assessments and attainment targets will comprise.

WHAT DO YOU DO WHEN THINGS GO WRONG?

The one major function which schools have is to provide each child with the best education possible according to his or her individual needs. But helping children to fulfill their intellectual potential is not their only purpose or aim.

Schools also have a vital role with regard to children's social, moral, emotional and physical welfare and development – thus helping each child to become a well-adjusted, well-rounded, caring and concerned human being. Learning the 'give and take' of life obviously happens within the family to a large extent, but it is at school that most of us first learn how to live within a larger, more impersonal community – how to value not only other people but ourselves as individuals within the group.

Ask any parent what they want for their child and, taking good health for granted, answers would range from confidence, compassion and contentment to success and satisfaction. We have expectations of our children and, in turn, expectations of their schools.

Surveys have shown that the vast majority of parents are, on the whole, satisfied with the schools their children attend – even if there are aspects which they would like to see improved such as having smaller classes or better facilities and resources. Inevitably, however, there are times when things go wrong.

Do you have special skills to offer your child's school?

Possible problems
- Reluctance to go to school
- Lack of progress in particular subjects
- Too much/too little homework
- Boredom
- Problems with a particular teacher
- Bullying
- Your child feels unfairly disciplined

Your major link with the school is your child and, therefore, your perception of the school is largely coloured by what she says. For teachers, your child is only one of many and things that affect her deeply may pass unnoticed.

> *The secret of dealing with problems is good communication between home and school!*

You won't solve a problem if:
- You hope that it will resolve itself
- You are reluctant to 'make a fuss'
- You believe your child is 'exaggerating'

Or if:
- You rush straight up to the school
- You accept without question everything your child says

All these reactions are very understandable, but they are unlikely to achieve a great deal! So what is the best way of tackling things? Look at our list of do's and don'ts.

In the unlikely event that things cannot be sorted out at school, the next step is to contact the local education authority. Telephone the LEA offices and ask for the name of your area education officer, or, failing that, the director of education. Then outline the problem in writing. He will make sure your letter is dealt with by the right person.

The final step, which is obviously for only the most serious of complaints, is to write to the Secretary of State for Education and Science. Some parents experiencing difficulties within the system have also successfully involved local MPs or councillors in investigating and supporting their complaints.

YOUR RIGHTS

- The 1980 Education Act gave parents the right to name the school they would prefer their child to attend. This preference can be refused only in strictly defined circumstances such as the school being full. Parents who are not satisfied were given the right to appeal to an independent appeals committee by this Act. The new Education Act of 1988

Choosing THE RIGHT SCHOOL

When it comes to choosing the right school for your child, you are quite likely to be beset with conflicting advice from family, friends and other parents. It can be helpful to hear what the parents say about a particular school, but local gossip can often be unreliable!

The most important and useful thing you can do is to arrange a visit to a potential school. Every school has a prospectus and it is a good idea to ask for one at the time you arrange your visit. Having visited a school, you will probably have an instinctive feel as to whether or not it is right for your child... trust your instincts!

Don't feel awkward or hesitant about asking questions. You are a consumer and help to fund the education system – you have a right to know what is on offer!

Many parents find it helpful to follow the plan below when choosing schools.

* List all the points you want to see in a school you think would be right for your child. We've suggested some. There are bound to be others.

* Talk it over with your child. Amend list if necessary.

* Send for school prospectuses and arrange appointments to visit.

* Visit – armed with the questions you would like answered.

* Go back to your list – how many ticks could you put on it? Are there any plus points (or negatives) which have arisen because of your visit that you may not have thought of to begin with?

THE LAST WORD...
No school is perfect and no school is all bad!

Some points to notice about any school

? Is there litter around the school premises?

? How do children behave generally in the playground? What is the level of supervision?

? What is the entrance hall/reception area like? Is there a welcoming feel with displays of work, for example?

? Are there other displays of work in evidence around the school? Do they look as if they have been there for months?

Primary schools

? What is the school's approach to the teaching of the following key subjects?
● reading ● writing
● maths ● science
Be wary of vague or evasive answers to your questions!

? Does the school have a partnership arrangement with parents e.g. for paired reading? (See page 29.)

Secondary schools

? What arrangements are made to help pupils settle in?

? What pastoral care system is in operation?

? Is there a policy of:
mixed ability teaching?
(all pupils taught together regardless of ability)
streaming?
(pupils placed in classes according to ability/attainment)
setting/banding?
(some subjects taught in ability/attainment groups)

? What is the policy with regard to homework?

? Is there a library? Is it an inviting place with books in reasonable condition which are well displayed?

? What other special facilities does the school have? (Hall? Gym? Laboratories? Swimming pool? Pottery room? etc.)

? If you see children in the classrooms, do they appear to be working purposefully and reasonably quietly?

? Do the head teacher and any staff you meet seem lively and genuinely interested?

? What arrangements are made for 'high fliers' and children experiencing any difficulty with, for example, reading? It's worth asking this question even if neither category fits your child; the school which cannot tell you its policy or practice probably *has* no policy and is, therefore, likely to be failing to meet the needs of *all* its pupils.

? What club or out of school activities are on offer?

? What kind of curriculum is provided during the first years? Is there a good breadth of subjects?

? At what age do 'options' operate? (Options are the choice to take on or drop various subjects.) What options are available?

? Is there a good work experience and careers counselling programme for all pupils which gives equal opportunities regardless of pupils' ability, gender, race and social background?

? On what basis are pupils entered for public examinations?

? Is it the sort of school you would have liked to have gone to?

Do / Don't	
Do Discuss the problem calmly and quietly with your child at an appropriate time (not in front of brothers or sisters or when a favourite TV programme is on). Look at page 8 for advice on helping your child to discuss things with you. Make a note of what your child has said to serve as a reminder if this seems appropriate.	**Don't** 'Interrogate' or 'accuse' your child or make hasty decisions and statements about who is at fault. Do it in front of the child.
Do Telephone the school to make an appointment to see the most appropriate person. In a primary school, see the class teacher first, and then the head. In secondary schools see the head of year or form/pastoral tutor. If you have to give a reason, simply say you are worried and would like to discuss a problem concerning your son or daughter. Alternatively, you could write a letter outlining the problem and then asking for an appointment to discuss it. This does have the advantage of giving the person time to get any facts or information together before your visit.	**Don't** Go to the school without an appointment because: (a) the person may not be available and you will have wasted your time, (b) it is highly unlikely that there will be sufficient time to talk to the person in any case.
Do Think about what you want to say and the questions you may want to ask before your visit. Jot them down.	**Don't** Make accusations; rather, say that your child has told you . . . and you felt the staff would want to know . . .
Do Make your discussion at the school a worthwhile one by: **remembering** that you are *both* concerned with your child's welfare; **outlining** the information you have been given or your view of the problem clearly and as concisely as possible; **remaining** calm and polite; **asking** what the school can do to help or cure the problem; **asking** what you can do to support any action taken by the school and when you can meet again to discuss progress. Make notes of what has been said when you get home. If the problem is a serious one which requires further or 'higher' action, it is sensible for you to keep your own record of any discussions and contact with the school. Consider how much your child needs to know about the discussion and proposed solutions. Obviously, this will depend both on your child and the nature of the problem, but a good rule of thumb is; enough to reassure but not enough to worry.	**Don't** Be surprised if the school was not aware of the problem; teachers have many pupils to deal with. Lose your temper (one always achieves more by diplomacy than with drawn daggers!). Simply accept what is said to you without question if you feel you are not getting all the facts or are told something you suspect is inaccurate. Be reluctant to ask who else you could discuss the problem with if you feel you aren't really getting anywhere.

prevents LEAs from artificially restricting the number of places available at a school.
- Parents have a legal right to withdraw their child from religious education lessons, or, alternatively, to complain if they feel that the school is not meeting its obligation to provide RE.
- Parents have no legal rights to control the choice of subject options, assignment to an examination class or to an ability stream. Most schools, however, are only too willing to discuss these aspects with parents.
- The 1981 Education Act concerning children with **special educational needs** gave parents new rights. The process of determining provision for children with special needs is quite complex and includes a formal assessment procedure to which parents may contribute. LEAs automatically provide information for parents about this.
- While it is an offence not to send your child to school under normal circumstances, the law does allow parents the right to educate their child at home providing it can be proved that the child is receiving an adequate and satisfactory education. The organisation *Education Otherwise* (see page 71) will provide information about this.
- The Sex Discrimination Act of 1975 made it illegal to exclude pupils from a subject *purely* on the grounds of gender. This means, for example, that subjects like woodwork or metalwork have to be available to girls as well as boys should they wish to take them up.
- Parents have to be represented on a school's board of governors. The 1986 Education Act strengthened the governors' role in the running of a school and they are directly accountable to parents through an annual report and meeting. The powers of school governors will be further increased by April 1993; that is the date by which all LEAs must hand over local financial management to schools. This means that the head teachers and governors of all secondary schools and at least all primary schools with 200 or more pupils will have control of their given expenditure budget instead of the LEA. (It will cover such items as staff salaries, rent and rates, books, equipment, examination fees and day to day premises costs – excluding capital expenditure.)

Your LEA should be able to give you more detailed advice concerning your rights as a parent.

HOW TO GET MORE INVOLVED

HELPING OUT IN SCHOOL

Schools do vary a great deal with regard to the amount of in-school support from parents that they encourage. There is more involvement at primary level. Parents can help in many ways.

The extra pair of hands for example:
- helping out with cooking, craft or computers
- going along on school trips
- covering books or helping to make teaching games/apparatus
- helping out with school sports teams.

Helping with literacy and language Many schools have parental involvement projects to aid children's reading and language skills. These work in a variety of ways, for example:

- a regular commitment from a parent to carry out paired/shared reading together at home each evening with their child
- going into school to talk, read stories or play reading games with two or three children (under the teacher's supervision)
- in a few areas of the country (*only* a few, e.g. London and Bristol) there are Volunteer Reading projects which involve anyone with the time to make a regular commitment going into a couple of schools – not where their own children attend. Here they work with individual children, sharing stories, talking or playing reading games. Training is provided for the volunteer tutors.

FUND-RAISING

Where *would* our primary and secondary schools be without the additional funds raised by parents! Fund-raising activities (fêtes, jumble sales, dances, car boot sales, raffles, sponsored events and so on) can be hard work but fun. They offer the chance to get to know other parents and to provide many things that the school cannot afford out of its normal allowances.

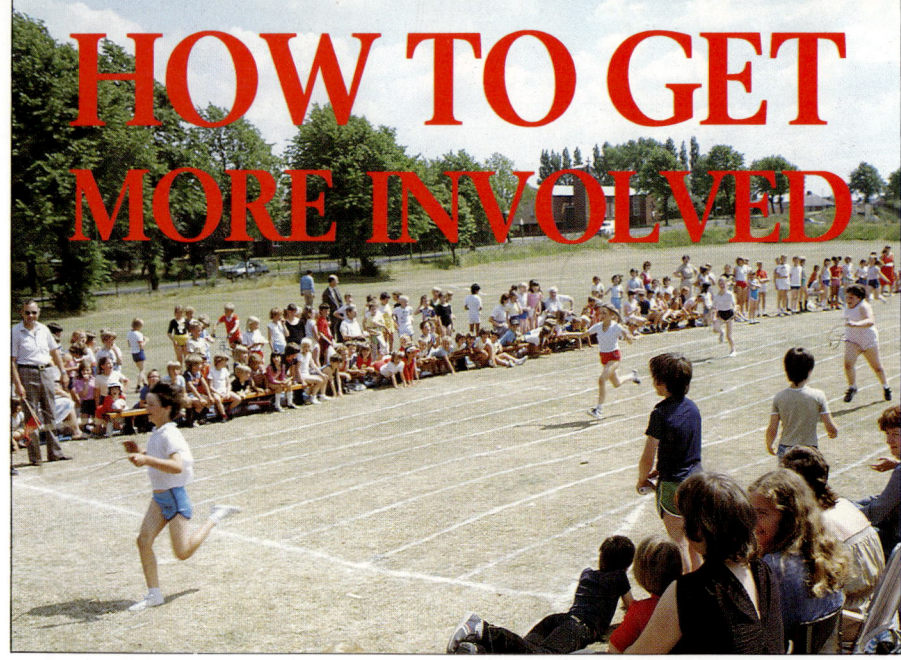

Do try to support events taking place in school. The school needs your support and so does your child.

PARENT TEACHER ASSOCIATIONS

Fund-raising is generally a major function of a PTA and, via the organisation, parents have a say in how the money is to be spent. What usually happens is that the head teacher and staff identify an area of need and suggest how the money might be spent. The PTA then agree or make other suggestions.

Schools with active PTAs or other parent/school organisations usually provide what are often known as curriculum evenings as well as social events. Sometimes the curriculum evenings will be instigated by the school and might be, for example, when the school's new core reading scheme or the approach to maths/science teaching is demonstrated and explained. Occasionally, there might be an outside speaker who will talk to parents and staff on a particular topic. The PTA, of course, can suggest to a head teacher that they would welcome a meeting to consider a specific topic of interest to parents.

Like any other association, PTAs often find it difficult to find or persuade people to serve on committees – this *can* be a very rewarding activity and nothing like as daunting as one might assume!

PARENT GOVERNORS

All governing bodies of schools now have parent governors as part of their number. Almost anyone can be a school governor – as long as they have not served a recent prison term or been bankrupt. Governing bodies include people nominated by the LEA, the head teacher, teacher representatives and co-opted members from the local community, businesses and so on. Parent governors are elected by the parents and must cease to hold office when they no longer have a child at the school.

Duties and responsibilities of parent governors

Before the 1988 Education Reform Act, the duties of governors included:
- allocating the school budget
- deciding on the school's sex education policy
- helping to select and appoint staff, including the head
- setting curriculum objectives
- deciding whether individual pupils should be suspended

After the 1988 Education Reform Act, the duties are extended to include the following, for schools with more than 200 pupils:
- responsibility, with the head, for managing the school's total budget
- determining staffing levels
- recruiting and promoting teachers
- making sure the requirements of the national curriculum are met

To be effective, governors must be prepared to make regular visits to the school, to see it in action, and must attend *at least* one meeting a term.

Following the Act, teacher and parent governors will, together, have more influence than political nominees on the governing bodies.

Parent governors will normally serve for four years.

The governors of a school play an important part in its life and running and, with the new Education Act, their powers are further increased. Being a parent governor allows you the opportunity of playing a significant part in the education of the children. Parent governors are the voice of the parents as a whole.

Many parents feel they would have little to contribute to a group of people whom they see as experts in education. There is no need to feel this: **parent governors are not expected to be experts in education – their expertise is as parents**. As such their contribution to meetings and discussions is from a different, but just as valid, point of view from any other governor.

Another reason for being reluctant to stand is not being sure what to expect. Again, fear of the unknown is worse than the reality! The LEA will provide new governors with information; some LEAs run courses and there is also an Open University course available.

OTHER LINKS BETWEEN HOME AND SCHOOL

Even if you don't have time or don't want to become involved with the school in the ways outlined above, there are still important links to be maintained which can only help your child.

PARENTS' OR OPEN EVENINGS

❝You never get to see the ones you really want to see – they don't turn up.❞

Do try to attend these; not only does it demonstrate to the teaching staff *and* your child that you are interested in her progress and education, but it is also an important opportunity to talk to your child's teacher(s) and see for yourself the work that has been done.

Where Parents' Evenings follow on from school reports, it is an opportunity to discuss and 'flesh out' the report. By doing this, you will know better how to follow it up at home – whether your child needs a hand in pulling up her socks, some reassurance, praise, a boost to confidence or whatever.

OCCASIONAL EVENTS

◆ Do make the effort to turn up to events such as concerts, Carol Services, sports days, plays and so on. **Your child may not appear to mind if you don't turn up, but any teacher would tell you that this is rarely the case.**
◆ Major events, such as concerts or plays, often take place in the evenings, making it very much easier for the working parent to attend.
◆ Take advantage of as many home-school links as possible!
◆ Praise and show your pleasure in anything in which your child takes part.

BUT WHAT IF THERE IS NO PTA?

There are some schools, still, which do not have PTAs or much in the way of events for parents. If one talks to the head teacher and staff of such schools, two reasons for this are usually given: either staff feel that the parents as a whole would not be sufficiently interested, or they are afraid that parents would exert too much pressure and try to influence unduly the running of the school. This is a negative and frustrating attitude, but it is up to parents to prove the school wrong.

One parent alone cannot change things; there may be many parents who feel they want to be more involved but don't know what to do about it. If you are in this situation, you might like to consider trying the following:

1 Talk to other parents, see if they feel it would be a good idea to have a PTA or a *Friends of ------- School* organisation. (A PTA needs the head's permission, but a 'Friends' group doesn't.) How many of them would be prepared to attend an informal meeting at your home to discuss it? Try to involve the parent governors.

2 Decide *why* you want such an organisation. Talk to friends who have children in other schools where there are good home-school links to find out what happens and what is achieved there. As a group, list the advantages you think there would be both for parents and for the school. Concentrate on the positive possibilities and don't waste precious time and energy on any current negative aspects and feelings!

3 Ask the parent governor(s) to raise the subject at the next Governors' meeting and make sure they have the results of your discussions and list of advantages (couched in 'asking politely' rather than 'demanding' tones). It would, it goes without saying, be sensible to let the head teacher know about the parents' wishes and that the parent governors are going to place this on the agenda.

4 DO REMEMBER The above step may not be necessary if the head teacher and staff have never done anything because they feel the parents wouldn't be interested or because they have tried and failed in the past. If that is the case, discussions with the head teacher by a group of parents should be all that is necessary to get things going. If the head teacher suggests a trial meeting to 'test the water' (a sensible idea), do your utmost to persuade as many parents as possible to attend!

❝Parents working in partnership with the school can only be of benefit to the children.❞

Praise anything in which your child takes part. Don't criticise, even if the violins did play off-key!

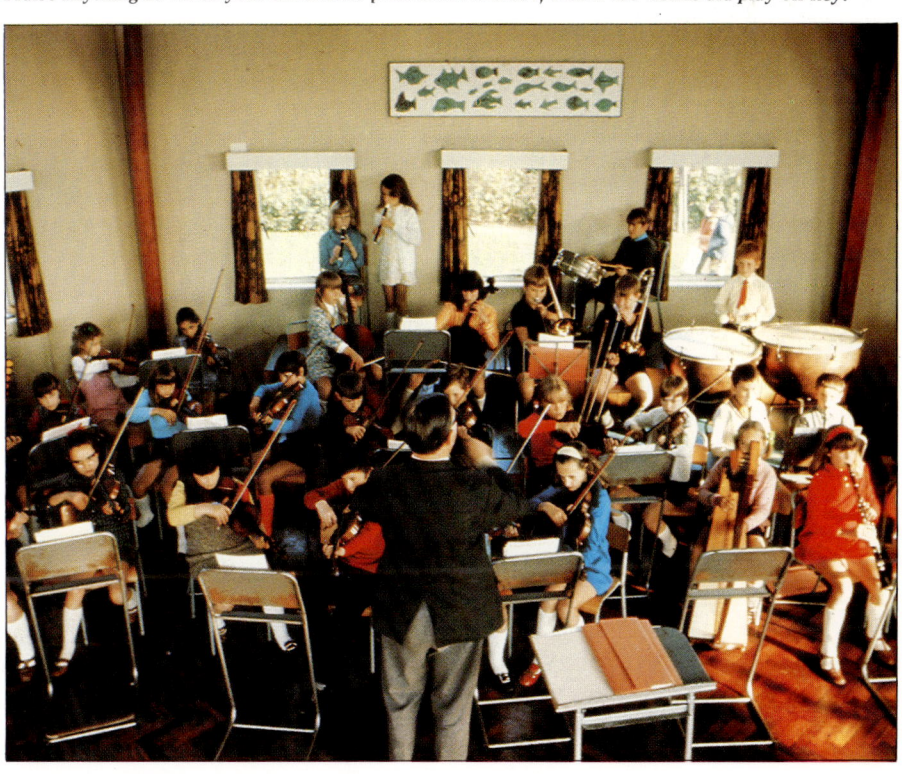

where to get

FURTHER READING

BOOKS

Bruno Bettleheim *A Good Enough Parent* Thames and Hudson

❛*A book to inspire and encourage every parent.*❜

Boston Women's Health Book Collective (edited by Michele Cohen and Tina Reid) *Ourselves and our Children* Penguin Books

❛*The chapter on 'The Middle Years' is full of practical advice, humour and personal examples of parents coping with bringing up and educating children.*❜

Barbara Bullivant *You are the Governor: How to be Effective in your Local School* National Council for Voluntary Organisations (available from bookshops)

Alan Graham *Help your child with Maths* Fontana

❛*Even if you find maths a problem yourself, this simple book will provide useful guidance on helping your child.*❜

K.P. Goldberg *The Parent's Book on Calculators* Oxford University Press

John Holt *How Children Fail; Escape from Childhood; How Children Learn* all Penguin Books

❛*Three excellent books which offer insights into how emotional and social factors affect children's learning.*❜

David Lewis *How to be a Gifted Parent; You can Teach Your Child Intelligence; Mind Skills* Souvenir Press

❛*Three practical guides on intellectual development.*❜

David Lewis *Helping your Anxious Child* Methuen

❛*Explores the effects of anxiety on classroom attainment and offers practical procedures for reducing it at particularly stressful times, like during exams.*❜

Terry Mahoney *Governing Schools: Powers, Issues and Practice* Macmillan Education

❛*Terry Mahoney seems to have a real 'feel' for the subject. Besides being sound and comprehensive, it is lively, entertaining and not afraid to use real, interesting cases to illustrate discussions of the proper role and practice of governing bodies.*❜

Peter Mortimore *School Matters: The Junior Years* Open Books

M. O'Connor *A Parent's Guide to Education* Fontana

Bonnie Remsberg and Antoinette Saunders *Help Your Child Cope with Stress*

❛*Offers sound guidance on helping children through stress.*❜

Geraldine Taylor *Be Your Child's Natural Teacher* Impact Books

Ted Wragg *Education – An Action Guide for Parents* BBC Publications

The Good Book Guide Braithwaite and Taylor

❛*An annual review for parents.*❜

For further information about parent governors, the following books may be helpful.
Joan Sallis *Parents and Governors* Routledge

Chris Lowe *The School Governor's Legal Guide* Croner Publications Ltd

MAGAZINES

Books for your Children

❛*Published three times a year. Available from Anne Wood Ed., P.O. Box 507, Harbourne, Birmingham B17 8PJ.*❜

Practical Parenting

❛*Family Circle Publications – available from supermarkets.*❜

Special Children

❛*For those concerned with children who have special educational needs. Available from Top Floor, 6/7 Hockley Hill, Birmingham B18 5AA.*❜

School Governor

❛*Intended for School Governors who want to be informed and effective. Available from Top Floor, 6/7 Hockley Hill, Birmingham B18 5AA.*❜

Times Educational Supplement

❛*Often has informative features on such subjects as school governors and the curriculum.*❜

GOVERNMENT REPORTS

There are many government reports that are worth looking at – for example, the subject working party reports on maths, science and English. These can be obtained from:

England National Curriculum Council, Room G1, Newcombe House, 45 Notting Hill Gate, London W11 3JB

Wales Schools Division 4, Welsh Office, Cathays Park, Cardiff CF1 3NQ

Also
The Taylor Report, A New Partnership for our Schools HMSO (information on governors)

The Warnock Report, Special Education Needs HMSO

The Cockcroft Report, Mathematics Counts HMSO

The Kingman Report, English HMSO

further advice

SOME USEFUL ADDRESSES

Advisory Centre for Education (ACE) publishes the magazine *'Where'* for parents, as well as booklets on educational issues like 'The Transfer from Primary to Secondary School'. Its address is 18 Victoria Park Square, London E2 9BP.

Association of Stammerers offers advice and contacts. Its address is c/o Finsbury Centre, Pine Street, London EC1R 0JH.

British Dyslexia Association refers individuals to nearest association where they can receive advice, support and therapy. Also issues information sheets and leaflets. Its address is Church Lane, Peppard, Oxfordshire RG9 5JN. Also The Dyslexia Institute, 133 Gresham Road, Staines TW18 2AJ.

Campaign for the Advancement of State Education (CASE) produces useful publications. Contact your local group via The Grove, High Street, Sawston, Cambridge CB2 4MJ.

College of Speech Therapists provides names of private therapists. Its address is: Harold Poster House, 6 Lechmere Road, London NW2.

Department of Education and Science (DES) is in charge of educational policy at national level. Its address is Elizabeth House, York Road, London SE1 7PH.

Education Otherwise is an organisation for parents who wish to educate their children themselves. Its address is 25 Common Lane, Hemingford Abbots, Cambridgeshire CE18 9AN.

Education Welfare Service This acts as a link between parents, the social services department and the school. Your local office will be listed under the local education authority section of your phone book.

Gingerbread is an organisation for single parent families, with local self-help groups. Its address is 35 Wellington Street, London WC2.

Home and School Council (publications only) is at 81 Rustlings Road, Sheffield S11 7AB.

Independent School Information Service (ISIS) will advise parents on private education. Its address is 56 Buckingham Gate, London SW1E 6AH.

Local Education Authority (LEA) You will find an address and telephone number for your local LEA in the phone book under the heading of your area e.g. 'Buckinghamshire LEA' or 'Solihull LEA'.

National Association for Gifted Children provides information and advice to parents who believe their children are in any way gifted. Its address is South Audley Street, London W1Y 5DQ.

National Confederation of Parent-Teacher Associations will advise on setting up and running a PTA. Their address is 43 Stonebridge Road, Northfleet, Gravesend, Kent.

Royal Association for Disability and Rehabilitation (RADAR) provides information on a large number of voluntary groups for children with special needs and their parents. Its address is 25 Mortimer Street, London W1N 8AB.

School Health Service You'll find their address in your phone book, under the heading of your local health authority (not your local education authority!).

School Psychological Service/Child Guidance See under the local education authority heading in your phone book. Educational psychologists employed by the LEA are responsible for, amongst other things, assessing children's educational difficulties. A request for assessment is usually made by the school.

The Scottish Parent-Teacher Council Its address is Atholl House, 2 Canning Street, Edinburgh EH3 8EG

USEFUL ADDRESSES FOR PARENT GOVERNORS

Action for Governors' Information and Training, c/o CEDC, Briton Road, Coventry CV2 4LF

National Association of Governors and Managers, 81 Rustlings Road, Sheffield S11 7AB

Open University, Governing Schools courses, Milton Keynes, Bucks MK7 6AA

Also available is a diagnostic report on your child from Dr David Lewis. See details on the next page.

DETAILED ASSESSMENT FOR YOUR CHILD

You can seek the help of a Diagnostic Report especially prepared for you by *Success!* consultant Dr David Lewis.

Dr Lewis has developed special diagnostic assessments which explore key aspects of classroom achievement. His detailed report offers you vital insights into your child's emotional and intellectual strengths and weaknesses.

There are eight assessments – each to be completed in your own home and at a pace to suit your child.

★ Motivation
★ Self image
★ Anxiety
★ General study skills

★ Reading
★ Handwriting
★ Spelling
★ Arithmetic

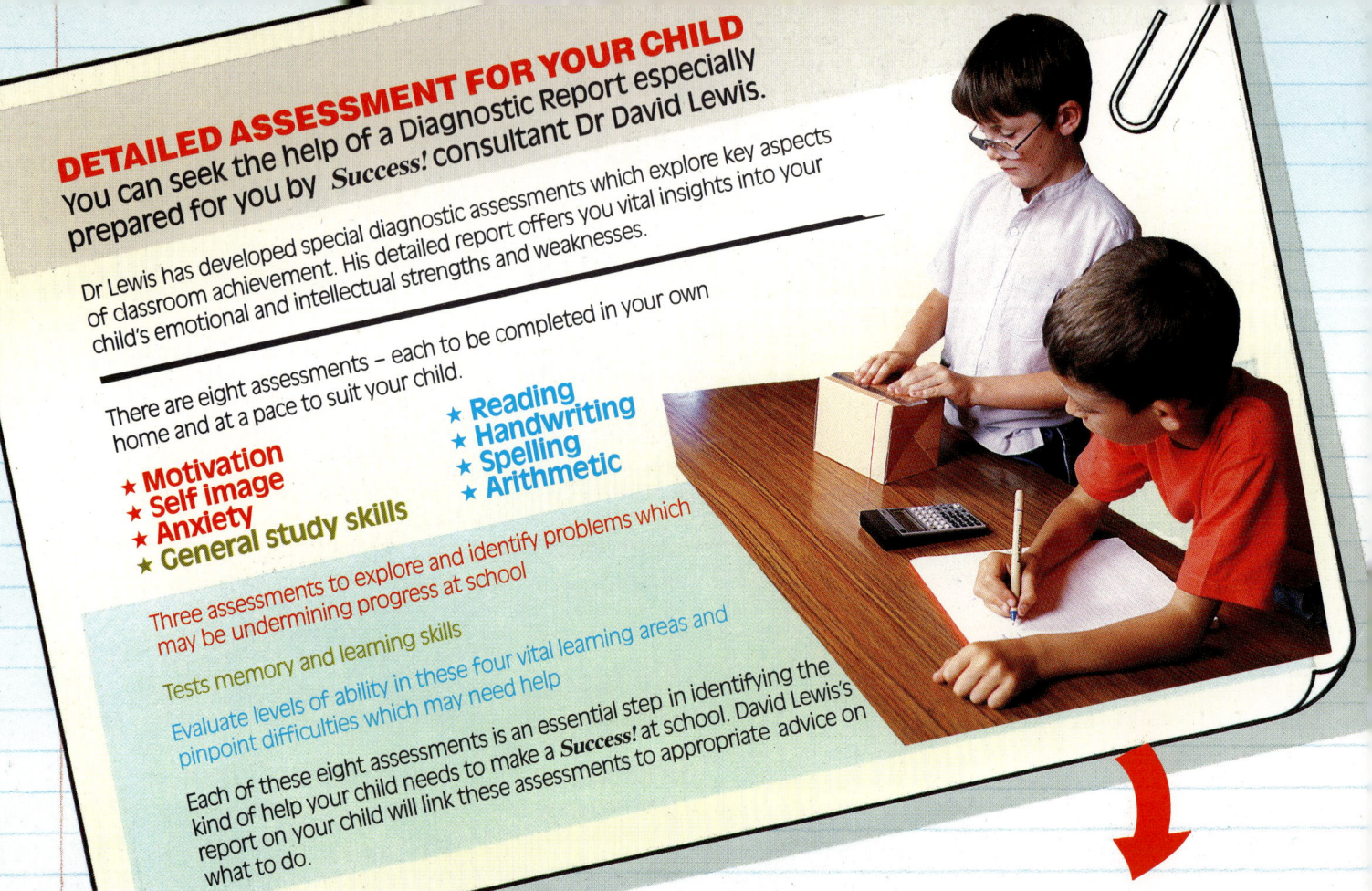

Three assessments to explore and identify problems which may be undermining progress at school

Tests memory and learning skills

Evaluate levels of ability in these four vital learning areas and pinpoint difficulties which may need help

Each of these eight assessments is an essential step in identifying the kind of help your child needs to make a *Success!* at school. David Lewis's report on your child will link these assessments to appropriate advice on what to do.

For **INFORMATION** on this unique service, please write to:
David Lewis BSc(Hons) D Phil, Darbies, East Dean, Eastbourne BN20 0BY

Where to find out about:

Arithmetical skills	38	Education Reform Act 1988	12, 62, 63, 66-67	Matching	25
Assessment	12, 22-23 (Reading), 30-31 (Writing), 62, 64, 72			Mathematical operations	38, 42, 43
Attainment targets	12, 64	Estimating	39, 43	Maths games	45
				Maths phobia	41
				Mental arithmetic	38, 44
				Mispronunciation	34
Bad language	56	Fear of failure	18	Mnemonics	11, 34
Bedrooms	55, 58	Filling the gaps	23, 29	Modelling	25
Body language	8	Fractional equivalents	44	Motivation	17
Bullying	50, 56, 66	Friendship	50		
				National curriculum	62, 63
				Neutral listening	8
				Note-taking	37
Calculators	39, 40, 42, 45	GIGO bank	54	Number bonds	38, 42, 43
Careful listening	8	Grammar	31, 33		
'Cliffhangers'	26			Over-motivation	18
Cloze	25				
Competence	53	Half-listening	8		
Comprehension questions	23, 25, 29	Handwriting	30, 33, 34	Paired reading	5, 29
		Home learning	6, 20, 57	Parent governors	68-69
Content (of writing)	31			Parent teacher associations	68, 69
Context building	28	Knowledge tree	10	Parents' evenings	60-61, 69
				Place value	43
				Predicting	23
DARTS (directed activities related to text)	25	Language games	37	Projects	12, 36
Decimals	39, 44	Language skills	27	Puberty	51
Drafting	36	Learning ladder	11	Punctuation	31, 33, 35
Dyslexia	37	Left-handers	35	Punishment	54

Reading aloud	22
Reading for enjoyment	26
Reading games	27
Relaxation	6, 49, 57
Religious education	63
Remembering:	
by place	11
what you read	23
Re-reading stories	29
Rewards	54
Rules	55
Scanning	29
Self-esteem	54
Self-image	52, 53
Sequencing	25
Skimming	29
Smoking	56
Spelling	31, 32, 33, 34
Spot messages	11
Stealing	56
Study, Cover, Write, Check	34
Success!	4, 5, 6, 20-21, 24-25, 32-33, 40-41
Tapes	11, 26, 3
Teachers	5, 60-61, 6
Television	26, 27, 5
Truancy	5

72